AMAZING
life together

INSPIRING LOVE STORIES
FROM ALL 50 STATES

LIZ & RYAN BOWER
founders of Amazing Life Together, a 501(c)(3) organization

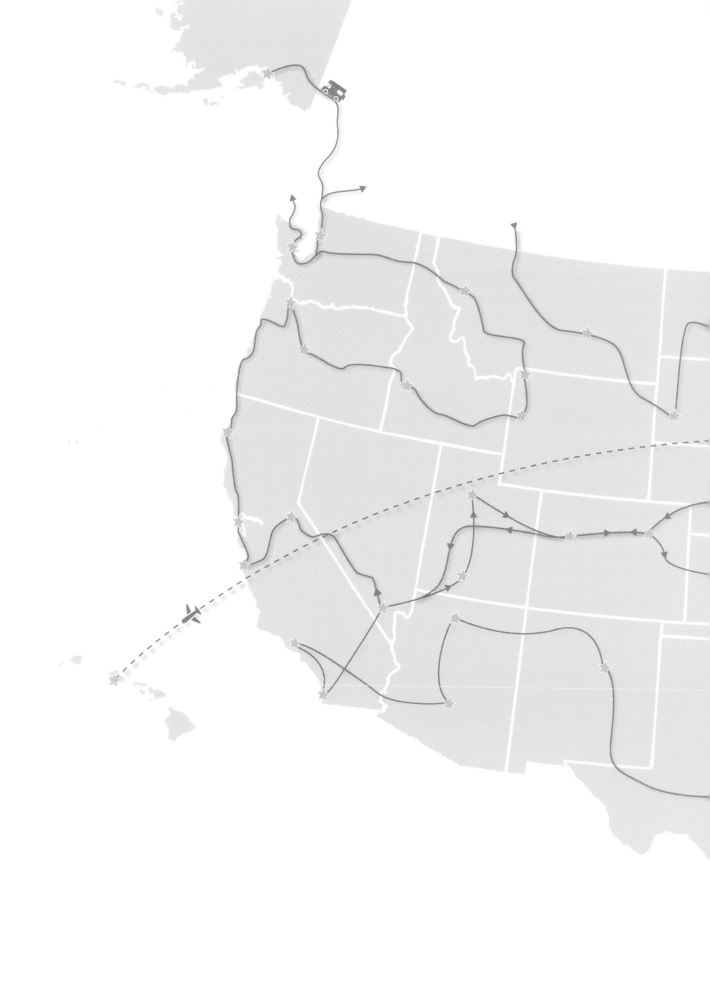

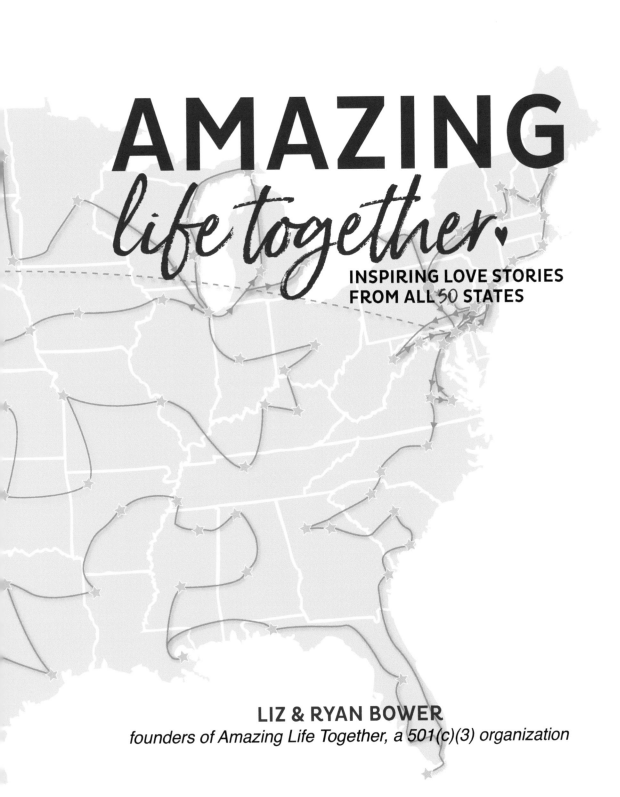

AMAZING
life together

**INSPIRING LOVE STORIES
FROM ALL 50 STATES**

LIZ & RYAN BOWER
founders of Amazing Life Together, a 501(c)(3) organization

For all of the couples we have had the honor of photographing in the past and will have the honor of photographing in the future. We are grateful for your love. ♥

Photography, Cover Design, and Book Design by:
Liz and Ryan Bower
www.lizandryan.com

Edited by:
Tina Solak and Jenna Camann

First Printing, 2017

ISBN 0-9986783-0-9 (Hardcover)
ISBN 0-9986783-1-7 (E-book)

Amazing Life Together
2700 Remington Ave. #415
Baltimore, MD 21211

www.amazinglifetogether.com

TABLE OF CONTENTS

INTRODUCTION

It was a warmer than usual Fall day on campus at Bucknell University. I had just completed an exam. I remember feeling distracted. My head was not in it, and I could feel in my gut that something was wrong.

As soon as class ended and I began my walk across campus to work in the Dean of Students Office, I received a call from my dad. He was a wreck. He could barely get words out. Immediately the tears began to flow from my eyes when I realized what was going on.

Eventually, my dad said, "Your mom left. There is a note on the table that says she is leaving and not coming back." As much as I didn't want to believe it, that morning, with a hand-written note on the table, my mom left my dad.

I remember making my way over to Rooke Chapel. I clearly was not in a state to go to work, and I just needed a place that was safe. I sat on the steps of the Chapel and just sobbed. After a frantic phone call where I couldn't get anything out, Ryan joined me. He rubbed my back and held me tight as the pain, anger, and frustration came out with every tear. It was like a waterfall pouring from my eyes.

Everything that I knew of marriage had just ended. Deleted... eliminated... stomped on. Divorce was always something that "happened to other families"... not mine. I was crushed in more ways than one.

It was hard. That experience of heartbreak was unlike anything we had ever experienced before. Ryan and I had been dating for four years at that point. Although my parents separation was certainly not what we had pictured would happen

in the months before Ryan proposed to me, we learned a lot about forgiveness, building trust, and loving unconditionally. We are confident that this was all part of God's plan for us. My parent's separation made it clear to us that we had to do the work to make sure our marriage was everlasting.

As high school sweethearts, we were married right out of college. We moved to Baltimore, Maryland and started our lives together. We did everything we thought we were supposed to do. We both had corporate jobs, attended Graduate School, bought a home and two cars, and spent more time working than we spent enjoying life together.

On January 1, 2009, we set a New Year's goal to start a business together and put our energy where we could hopefully make a meaningful impact on people's lives. We started a wedding photography business. We thought we were doing it because we loved taking photos and we loved being with couples on that crazy, beautiful, day of their lives. That is definitely true. But after years of photographing weddings, we realized there was a deeper reasoning behind why we do what we do.

In 2012, as we photographed one of our last weddings of the season, this why started to become clear. We were photographing our beautiful bride in her gorgeous white gown. She had her hair and makeup done, and it was about the time where she started to realize it was her wedding day. We were in the corner of the room where things were actually pretty quiet. As we captured bridal portraits and invited the bride to truly soak in the moment, she was suddenly interrupted. One of her bridesmaids came barreling into the room as if the world was going to end. She made quite the entrance as she exploded through the door, bare-naked. She was crying as she exclaimed, "why does this always happen to me?!"

The world was not ending. The drama she created on our sweet bride's wedding day, at the exact moment she was truly soaking in that she was about to say "I do," was simply because the zipper on her bridesmaid dress broke.

It was in that moment that we realized there is so much hype surrounding the wedding day and so little focus on the marriage afterwards. We wanted to change that.

Shortly after that wedding, we started Amazing Life Together. We had no idea what it would look like at the time, but we knew we had a passion in our hearts to do work that matters. To touch the lives of couples, not just on their wedding days, but beyond. Yes, wedding days are one of the happiest days of couples' lives. However, they are often surrounded by heartbreaking situations that are impossible for us to ignore. Families that refuse to talk to one another; families that don't even show up; families that arrive just in time for the ceremony and leave as soon as they can because the awkward tension is just "too much to handle." On a day that is supposed to be so full of love, it is often clouded by so many distractions.

The reality is, the world needs more love! We are definitely not the only ones who need positive examples of marriage in our lives!

In 2014, we had a particularly challenging year. We witnessed our families go through super challenging situations (addiction, illnesses, divorce, etc.). I went through my own health scares, resulting in two surgeries. We were struggling with the tension of our wedding photography business, where we felt passion in our hearts to work as wedding photographers and capture this incredibly meaningful day in our couple's lives, but felt a passion even greater to do more. We were feeling comfortable in our home, but a crazy uncomfortableness of "settling" in the excessiveness that society expects of us. We craved community, but recognized that our community was spread all over the world.

After having very similar hard conversations over and over again, Ryan finally said, "look, we have to do something about this!"

So, we decided to go on an Amazing Marriage Adventure, where we would travel to all 50 states in search of inspiring love stories that we could document and share. Within a few months of that transformative conversation, we rented out our home in Baltimore, bought an RV, and started on the Adventure. Over a 13 month period, we drove to 49 states, including Alaska, and flew to Hawaii as our 50th state. We interviewed over 95 couples, 76 of which are included in this book, and were blown away by the stories they shared with us.

Throughout the Adventure, we knew in our hearts we were exactly where we were suppose to be. So many couples poured their hearts out to us, and it was our responsibility to share these stories with the world. We all need more love in our lives and it is an honor to be able to share this experience with you. We hope these stories from real couples fill your heart with love, hope, and inspiration, as they did ours. Life is an adventure, lets make it amazing together. ♥

AMAZING ≠ PERFECT

When we first started the Amazing Marriage Adventure, we were in search of the "perfect" couple from every state. We had a vision in our minds of this sweet old couple we saw guiding each other through the crowds of Rockefeller Center in New York City during Christmas time one year: the gentlemen with a cane, holding onto his wife's shoulder as they wandered through the crowd blissfully. Among the hundreds of thousands of people, they acted as if they were the only people around.

With that vision in our minds, we were not thinking about what they had been through to get to that point in their lives. We just pictured how "perfect" it was that they were so beautifully in love.

After meeting just a few couples on this journey, we quickly came to realize that the idea of a "perfect" couple does not exist. The reality is, life can be challenging at times. The world that we dream about as kids, where everything goes as planned and everyone is happy all of the time, is simply not a reality. The reality is, that sweet old couple in New York City had to work through a lot of challenges and hurdles in their lifetime to walk in front of us to see the Rockefeller Christmas Tree that day.

The stories that couples shared with us across the United States changed our perspective on what an amazing marriage looks like. Many of the stories these couples shared with us involve heartbreaking experiences that one could never imagine going through. Many of these couples have gone through, or continue to go through incredible challenges, like fighting a terminal illness, losing a child, infertility, financial failures, etc.

Often times, we were introduced to these couples through a nomination form from our website. The nominators often shared their perspective of the couple they were nominating in a similar way that we described that sweet old couple in Rockefeller Center. From the outside, you would never know they had been through. But, when you

learn more about their story, you realize there is so much more that has led to their amazing marriage today.

It is so incredibly easy to look around and think everyone else has it perfect. Especially with social media so readily available at our finger tips. It is easy to get lost in trying to be "perfect" when "perfect" truly doesn't exist.

After meeting with close to 100 couples on this Amazing Marriage Adventure, living an Amazing Life Together has taken on a whole new meaning to us. When we think about living an amazing life together, we envision embracing the challenging times and appreciating every moment that we have together. We believe that life is not perfect. In fact, it is through the challenges that we become who we are. We have the option to let them weigh us down, or embrace them to build us up to be better together.

Watching my parents fall out of love, opened our eyes to the wholehearted investment needed to have an everlasting marriage. It was not easy to experience the heartbreak of that situation for my mom, dad, and family, but it certainly has lead us all to truly appreciate the hard work that comes with marriage. We may not fully ever truly understand the decisions that were made on that Fall day, but we are grateful to know it has lead to undiscovered happiness and a deeper understanding of love for my mom, dad, and family.

We hope that whatever challenge life throws your way today, or in the future, that you take a moment to appreciate that exact moment. It may not be easy to appreciate the hard times, but have faith in knowing, it is part of your amazing story. We hope this book is a constant reminder and inspiration to live an amazing life together. ♥

"When we think about living an amazing life together, we envision embracing the challenging times and appreciating every moment that we have together. We believe that life is not perfect. In fact, it is through the challenges that we become who we are. We have the option to let them weigh us down, or embrace them to build us up to be better together."

A QUICK NOTE

One of our favorite quotes from this Adventure that touched us deep in our hearts was from Shireen and Nick, who we met in Salt Lake City, Utah. They said, "There is no right way to do life. There are a lot of right ways to do life."

Each individual story in this book is unique, and we believe has the ability to inspire love. We do understand everyone has their own beliefs of what marriage should look like. However, we believe it is not our duty to judge others, but our opportunity to open our hearts and be inspired by a unique perspective of love. ♥

TERA *and* WES

MARRIED 7 YEARS
FLORENCE, ALABAMA

Tera and Wes met in college. Both were coming out of serious relationships. They met one evening while out with a group of friends and from across the room, Wes and his orange polo shirt stood out to Tera. "In that instant, it felt like a light switched on in my heart... almost literally. I knew he was to be my husband."

After a summer of fun together, Tera was certain marriage was the next step in their path. However, Wes wasn't quite ready to even think about the future. He broke up with Tera. Although devastated, the breakup forced Tera to think about herself and who she was as an individual. "I didn't realize then how much I needed to work on my heart before I could be with someone else."

They spent a year apart pursuing opportunities that took them miles away from each other. When they reunited in the summer, their friendship blossomed.

It wasn't until Wes accepted a job more than two hours away from Tera, that he realized just how special Tera was in his life. "Once he realized he would lose me, he made it official. I was finally his, and just over a year later, we were married."

In the eight years Tera and Wes have been married, they have travelled the world together, visiting more than 20 countries. They have built a business from the ground up, which has

sustained their family for almost nine years. They have two amazing children and recently simplified their lives by moving into a 650 sq. ft. home.

"The overall theme of our marriage is adventure. Which, I never thought would be the theme of my marriage. I was so straight and narrow and definitely saw myself as a housewife. Wes has opened up the entire world to me and showed me that anything is possible."

With adventure, often comes more opportunity for struggle. "We've set ourselves up for more failure and more potential to get lost along the way. We learned really early on, when there is a struggle, it is really easy to point fingers at the other person, or point the finger so hard at yourself that you ruin your own life. So, we have never allowed ourselves to point the finger. We are always carrying the burden together and that makes it a lot lighter for sure."

"Everything we do is a team effort. Everything. When I was pregnant, we talked about expectations for parenting. We made the conscious decision not to lose ourselves and our relationship during this season of life. It is very difficult and a constant battle not to. However, we know we need to lead by example so our kids can see the relationship we have. We want them to know that the world is open and anything is possible. The best way for them to see that is

to see it through us. We want them to see us fail. We want them to see when we struggle and when we succeed, so they can see how we handle it together. Hopefully, one day when they are in that position, they will know they are not alone in it. They have seen our example."

It is not always easy, but that is part of the adventure. "We know we need to always keep each other in check."

Tera and Wes summed it up best. "Never point the finger at each other. Always work together and be on each other's side. Talk about everything. EVERYTHING. Never give the other person a reason to not be able to trust you. If they trust you, they feel safe with you and that is key. Dance. Put a radio in your kitchen and dance every day."

"An amazing marriage is dreaming together and then working together to make it reality." ♥

"...we know we need to lead by example so our kids can see the relationship we have. We want them to know that the world is open and anything is possible. The best way for them to see that is to see it through us."

MATTYE *and* WOODY

MARRIED 3 YEARS
BIRMINGHAM, ALABAMA

"The secret to a happy marriage is also the hardest thing about marriage: to think of your spouse before yourself. It's not often our first reaction as humans to think of anyone before ourselves, but marriage is the place where we must commit to put this into practice time and time again. Marriage is this beautiful gift we're given, where we get to care for another heart all of our lives. The challenge is to care for that heart like I'd want someone to care for mine. We've found that when we serve each other in love, we find ourselves more in love. The more I think about Woody and consider him before myself, the more I find that I love and value him. Actions lead and feelings follow. By serving each other, we find ourselves in a happy marriage." ♥

ELISA *and* KEITH

MARRIED 2 YEARS
ANCHORAGE, ALASKA

"Our couple super power is cuddling. I feel
like it makes a lot of things better." ♥

BRI *and* KARRICK

MARRIED 4 MONTHS
ANCHORAGE, ALASKA

"Karrick and I met our freshman year of college at the University of Idaho. We were friends the first two years of college, and around the end of our sophomore year, we realized that there might be more to our friendship than we originally thought."

When Bri and Karrick returned to school for their junior year, they started to date. During the spring semester, Bri studied abroad in Spain. "Karrick surprised me with a ticket to visit over Spring Break. Needless to say, our junior year flew by and we fell more and more for each other all the way through senior year."

As they talked about their future together, they knew they were on the path towards marriage. "We had a lot of friends that got married right out of college, but we were never in a rush." Instead of focusing on planning their wedding, they decided to start their "adventure of a lifetime."

Following graduation, Karrick offered Bri three places to go: Anchorage, Seattle, or Hawaii. Bri said she knew Karrick wanted Anchorage. "So, I said, okay." Karrick received a job opportunity in Alaska and in 2011, they both headed north to start their careers.

"Moving to Alaska was like our version of moving to 'the big city.' Moving thousands of miles away from friends and family, and only having each other, was a huge risk."

Karrick's job as an engineer, working for an oil company, required him to spend some time on the North Slope in the oil fields. During the first two years of living in Alaska together, Karrick had rotations where he spent two weeks in the oil fields and two weeks at home.

"That was definitely hard because we were really excited. We had just moved up here, got our first apartment together, and it was really awesome. Then, all of sudden, they told us Karrick had to start a slope rotation in a week. I remember not really comprehending that until he was gone for the first time."

"I think the first year was a little rougher than we had planned. It was really hard to be far away from friends and family. I learned a lot about patience and had to realize, he wasn't doing it to me; he was doing it for his job." The distance also taught them a lot about communication. "We've both had to make communication a priority and make sure that we aren't neglecting one another due to any miles between us."

A few years after making the move to Alaska, buying their first home, and welcoming their "four-legged sidekick, Miller," to the family, Bri and Karrick married in Spokane, Washington.

"Now that we are married, I feel a lot more content. I am not so worried about the future, because I know that Karrick is right there with me. We are going to get through it no matter what."

"We have definitely made a life here together. We have a good base of friends that are basically family at this point."

"Our best piece of advice for other couples is to not be afraid to go on a new adventure together. You might be surprised how fun it is. I get really nervous about change, in general, and I think moving to Alaska has taught us to be more go-with-the-flow. Never take things too seriously.

We've learned throughout our relationship that there's a lot to be thankful for and the small things really don't matter in the grand scheme of things."

"We love having companionship, and knowing that we have someone always there for us means more than anything. Being able to experience life together is one of the most exciting things to look forward to."

"An amazing marriage to us is always having our adventure buddy/best friend by our sides." ♥

"We've learned throughout our relationship that there's a lot to be thankful for and the small things really don't matter in the grand scheme of things."

DELPHIA *and* MATT

MARRIED 1 YEAR
ANCHORAGE, ALASKA

"An amazing marriage is never losing sight of what is important. Don't sweat the small stuff and always leave room to grow." ♥

JEN *and* REUBEN

MARRIED 15 YEARS
PHOENIX, ARIZONA

Jen and Reuben met through a church activity. Reuben had just spent two years serving a mission for their church in Argentina and Jen was still in college. "My life to that point had been rocky. On the outside, I was an independent woman who was not willing to let the world break me down. Coming from a divorced and broken home, I learned very young that it was up to me to write the successes of my future. I was motivated to succeed and wasn't willing to let anything keep me from that. Reuben, on the other hand, came from a humble home with parents who had been married all his life. He was the second oldest of nine children. He was a little intimidated by my independence, and I was skeptical of the unconditional love he showed me at every turn."

Slowly he peeled back the layers of pain Jen carried from her childhood. Behind that front, Jen was a sponge waiting for love. Jen and Reuben were married one year after they met and are now the parents of four children.

"Reuben was super insecure when we were dating, and I was Miss Independent. When we were married, he was like, 'okay I have her.' He was no longer insecure and I, all of a sudden, became insecure. Through my insecurity, I would come to Reuben and say, 'I just need more from you.' I longed for that glow in his eyes, and some of that was kind of lost. I was longing for a stronger emotional connection."

"Years later, we realized that Reuben was showing me his love by doing the dishes, taking the kids, and giving me a night out. What I really wanted was Reuben right next to me, talking and connecting with me, and holding me. We realized he was loving me with his love language,* not mine. Once we made this realization, our love languages were more matched."

"Our love is strong and unique because we have never allowed our trials to dictate our love. We have never settled for substandard. We would never accept distance as a way of being. We never gave up on the notion that great love comes with sacrifice, love, and perseverance. We always seek refuge through each other. We always work together to look at the challenges we have and make mutual goals in how we can help each other overcome them. Oftentimes, that means having difficult conversations. Sometimes, that means creating more time for each other, or respecting the other person's need to have alone time. As we have worked to perfect our love, what we have learned is that life doesn't have to be perfect to be beautiful. The reality is, perfect for us is just having each other by our sides through it all."

To celebrate their anniversary each year, Jen and Reuben set aside time to get away together. On their 15th Anniversary, they spent a few days in Sedona, Arizona. Making the most of their time away together, Jen came prepared with

The 5 Love Languages by Gary Chapman

conversation starters, music to dance to, and a plan to go visit Schnebly Hill, the place they shared their first conversation about marriage. "We did a lot of reminiscing. We hiked, explored, and talked. We talked, and talked, and talked, about things we did wrong and things we did right."

Their visit back to Schnebly Hill made a big impact on Reuben. "*I started remembering being that in love. I remember planning special dates and following through on it. I remember being* *excited, being intentional about it, and it being the only thing that I wanted to do.*"

"After our weekend away, our love grew one hundred fold. What was already great was magnified in a way I can't even articulate. My husband's eyes were open and he fell even more in love with me than he had ever been."

"It is so easy for couples to get distracted by life and forget to nurture and care for their marriage. It is easy to let the ways of work, children, finances,

and other distractions take us away from the most important relationship in our life. We tend to forget that our marriage and relationship needs to be nurtured and loved, for it to continue to grow and flourish. This quote by F. Burton Howard says it all:

'If you want something to last forever, you treat it differently. You shield it and protect it. You never abuse it. You don't expose it to the elements. You don't make it common or ordinary. If it ever becomes tarnished, you lovingly polish it until it gleams like new. It becomes special because you have made it so, and it grows more beautiful and precious as time goes by.'"

"It doesn't matter how short or long we've been married, it's never too late to rekindle that love like it once started." ♥

"As we have worked to perfect our love, what we have learned is that life doesn't have to be perfect to be beautiful. The reality is, perfect for us is just having each other by our sides through it all."

KYLIE *and* AARON

MARRIED 8 YEARS
GILBERT, ARIZONA

"Put God first. I believe that if we allow God to be the center of our relationship, he will make it much more beautiful, more rock-solid and more fun. The times that we left God out were usually not as rich. We believe He's the Creator who makes beautiful things out of our lives and can turn our messy selves (or messy relationship) into something good. You don't have to be churchy to do it, and it can even start with just one of you."

"Aaron has been God's gift to me, and I believe His reward for waiting for the right one to come along." ♥

BECCA *and* JON

MARRIED 1 YEAR
FAYETTEVILLE, ARKANSAS

Becca and Jon met while living in Washington, D.C. Becca was working on Capitol Hill and Jon was living in the suburbs, working in vehicle logistics. They were introduced to each other through a mutual friend during dinner. Jon thought the dinner was exactly that, a dinner with friends. However, Becca knew it was a setup. They ran into each other a few weeks later at an outdoor concert and then continued to see each other for the next several months.

"As we got to know each other, we discovered uncanny similarities and formed an inseparable bond." For Jon, "*Becca opened doors for fun and experiences in a new city.*" For Becca, "Jon was a grounding force in a chaotic city."

After a year of dating in D.C., Jon was relocated to Atlanta for work. Before leaving D.C., Becca and Jon talked about marriage and even went ring shopping. However, it was important to Jon that he did not feel pressured into proposing. "*Deciding when and who you marry, as a man, is one of the few decisions that I believe should be*

yours, free of pressure and constraints. That's the one call, and the most important decision, you're going to make in your whole life."

About six months into living hundreds of miles away from each other, Jon knew it was time to propose. "*I just woke up and was like 'This is it! It's time. We need to do this!'*" So, he bought the ring and planned a romantic evening the next time Becca was in town. "The proposal was beautiful and more romantic than I could have imagined."

Becca and Jon were married in Fayetteville, Arkansas. "The wedding day was crazy, but we made it a point to focus on each other and spend time together throughout the day. It was important for us to be gracious to our guests, but also to place the emphasis on our relationship and our marriage. I want to remember that feeling of us making eye contact when I walked down the aisle. If I can always get back to that, I think we'll be good!"

After the wedding, they continued to live long-distance for a few months before Becca moved to Atlanta. A few months later, Becca was offered an exciting job opportunity in Arkansas. "When I was deciding whether to take the job in Arkansas or stay in Atlanta, I received some great advice when I called Jon's dad for his perspective. I said, 'Am I a bad wife if I take this job and move?' And he said, 'First of all, let's just lose the term wife, and say spouse.' And that sort of put it into perspective for me and made me realize I had a traditional mindset. He said 'It's a trade off. You're equals in this journey, so make the decision that you think is best for your family, not what you feel obligated to do.'"

Becca took the job. They made the move to Northwest Arkansas and bought their first home together. Their move from the city to a small town, and from living apart to living together, has not been easy. "*We have struggled with giving up some of our independence as single people. Decisions we took for granted living separately, now have effects on each other. This has been one of the hardest things for me. Being a single guy taking care of myself, it was very easy to get set on my ways and think 'this is who I am and I'm not changing that.' But, when you enter into a marriage, there are things that you have to bend on. Bend so you don't break.*"

"Living with someone isn't always easy, but if you're gracious to your spouse and willing to compromise on some of your wants and needs, you are much better off. My spouse is more important than whatever this 'thing' is, so choose to let that thing go."

"An amazing marriage is sharing life's moments together and creating memories that are uniquely 'us.'" ♥

"...when you enter into a marriage, there are things that you have to bend on. Bend so you don't break."

NATALIE *and* BRENDON

MARRIED 13 YEARS
SANTA CRUZ, CALIFORNIA

Natalie and Brendon met on the school bus when they were in high school. Natalie was 14 years old and Brendon was 15 years old. "We became friends and talked all the time. My parents often commented how they had never heard two people talk so much. We started dating when Brendon turned 16 years old, with the understanding from my parents that we could date as long as he came to church with us."

Natalie and Brendon became best friends over the next few years and had a more meaningful relationship than most people their age. When Natalie went to college, Brendon noticed that their priorities were different. Natalie was ready to "strike out on her own." Brendon broke up with her. After dating for three years, their breakup was devastating to Natalie. They later came to terms that it was actually a good thing, because it helped Natalie realize how much she loved Brendon. "It really helped me set my priorities. I realized this is truly what I want and everything else is just meaningless."

They dated again for another year and decided to get married. Just two months after their engagement, Natalie and Brendon were married. "We were really excited about our wedding day and everything that comes with that, but we were more excited about our marriage."

"We love being married because we get to experience a closeness and relationship that is so special. Welcoming a spouse to help you through the good times and bad times, to know you better than anyone on the planet, to help you get over things even when it might mean receiving some honest advice or criticism, can be humbling."

"When we got married, I realized this isn't about me. I learned to prefer Brendon, and be selfless, even when I don't really want to be. It is for the better of our relationship. I want to look back on my life and know that I was a good wife to my husband. We only get one shot; this is my only chance."

Natalie and Brendon now have four kids. They try to take a walk every day by themselves, just to talk. "We've been best friends for 10 years before having kids. It would be weird not having those times together."

"It is very easy to get discouraged if you keep your eyes on the material things around you, and think that is all that there is." Natalie and Brendon make it a priority to always get to the root of the challenges they face, by making sure they are doing what they feel is important. They are constantly reevaluating by asking these questions: "What is really important in life; How do we spend our money; How do we spend our time; What do we teach and model for our children; How are we treating/serving others in our community?"

"When we walk humbly in our marriage, our needs are prioritized and met. Our marriage is built on the teachings of Jesus Christ and the Bible. When we follow those teachings, we have peace, unity, love, and respect in our marriage and family. When we lose sight of those, our relationships and life get chaotic and stressful, and we hurt others."

"Our faith has kept us focused on the fact that this life is but a vapor, ever fleeting. If we do not love and forgive others, we miss out on joy and peace and the best that is yet to come."

"One piece of advice we have for married couples is to continue to have sex. God created sex as a beautiful thing inside marriage. Sure, schedules are busy and some people are night owls while others are not, but meet the needs and desires of your spouse. That being said, meet your spouse's non-sexual needs too!" ♥

"We were really excited about our wedding day and everything that comes with that, but we were more excited about our marriage."

AMY *and* JAMES

MARRIED 14 YEARS
LAKEWOOD, COLORADO

James and Amy met in February, 1997 in Abilene, Texas. Amy was a sophomore at Abilene Christian University, and James was in his second year at a community college in New York, getting ready to transfer to Abilene. When he transferred, both Amy and James were in existing long-distance relationships. They spent a lot of time just hanging out as friends and establishing a great friendship.

About a year later, James showed up at Amy's apartment to tell her about his most recent breakup. He had a party he was planning to attend that weekend and eventually asked Amy to join him. "During the party, there was just a chemistry that hadn't been there before. By the end of the night, he had his arm around my shoulders as we watched the bonfire."

"Because I was raised in a Christian denomination that was far different from his, he had some serious cold feet regarding our relationship. He didn't want to lose our friendship and was scared we'd ruin everything if we dated. I recommended we just commit to not do that, and give dating a try. I really thought we had something. He agreed, and we had our first kiss that night."

"However, the very next day when he picked me up to run some errands, we were in the Walmart parking lot, and he started to break up with me. He said he just didn't think the difference in our theological beliefs would work. I told him that

when I said I wanted to give our relationship a shot, I was thinking we could try for more than 24 hours. I talked him out of the breakup, and from that day on, our relationship and love grew."

Amy and James spent much of the next six months studying the Bible together. They had a lot of arguments. But, working through that conflict helped them grow stronger. "We realized the fear of our differences in our beliefs was bigger than the differences itself."

A few months later, James proposed. Less than a year later, Amy and James were married.

"We had a lot of expectations going into marriage that we didn't realize we had. We did a lot of assuming and didn't ask questions. I don't think we knew very much about how to meet each other's needs. We had moved from Texas, where we knew everybody, to Denver, where we literally knew nobody. We had spent so much time together and had processed through so much, we just expected each other to read one another's mind."

"One of our larger obstacles was just simply how we dealt with conflict. We are both firstborns, and neither of us is afraid of yelling. Our arguments in the early years were pretty rough and ugly. We knew it wasn't okay. We definitely hurt each other. But, we worked on it, prayed together, made commitments to change, and we eventually became better at dealing with conflict in loving ways. We're still not perfect and do have arguments, but the volume and intensity are way more manageable than in those first years."

"We had a friendship as a foundation of our relationship. The friendship makes us more committed to work through the hard stuff. If we based our marriage on just marriage vows, by itself, there would be no heart connection. They would just be words."

"We are big believers that it is a daily choice to stay committed and stay working at it. There are days that we have not liked each other, but we have made a choice to be loving, even when we don't feel like it."

"As we approach the 15 year mark this summer, I'm not sure our relationship has ever been stronger. And that is something I prayed for us from the very beginning."

"An amazing marriage is worth fighting for." ♥

"We had a friendship as a foundation of our relationship. The friendship makes us more committed to work through the hard stuff. If we based our marriage on just marriage vows, by itself, there would be no heart connection. They would just be words."

ROHANNA *and* MICHAEL

MARRIED 7 MONTHS
NORWALK, CONNECTICUT

"I first saw Michael when I was 16 years old, the summer he moved to my small town in Connecticut. He rode past my car, and I remember asking my friend, 'Who is that boy?'" Rohanna saw him one additional time before running into him at the local grocery store. "I walked into work at the grocery store, and he was standing with the other trainees starting that day. I remember my heart speeding up, a teenage crush. Marriage was so outside of my realm of thinking at that time. I was just 16 years old."

Michael recalled, "*At that point I was just thinking to myself, she is funny. This seems like a good thing, so I am going to pursue it.*"

Rohanna and Michael started dating that Spring and she asked him to her Junior Prom that year. They dated throughout the rest of high school and decided to stay together when she moved to Washington, D.C. for college.

"It never really felt long-distance. It is what it is. We never put those labels on it. The distance was good for us. It was important to have that separation and allow ourselves to have our own space. Knowing that we still wanted to be together, after so many years of living hours apart, solidified our decisions about our future."

During Rohanna's graduation weekend from college, Michael took her out to dinner and gave her a key, asking her to move in with him. She moved back to Connecticut, and they found an apartment together.

"We started talking about marriage after we started living together. He asked me to marry him in our living room, in the home we had built together. It was perfect."

"Ethnically, we both identify as first generation Americans. We just get each other. Family expectations, the importance of staying connected to our home country that we don't even understand, and feeling so American even when our families still want to hold onto their home culture, are all challenges we identify. We don't have to talk about it, we just understand each other."

"I think we are still trying to figure out what our family looks like. We come from different cultures and different religious backgrounds, and both of us are kind of hardheaded about those things. With maturity though, things change, and we are more willing to hear each other. I think about which parts of me will blend into our future together, and which I will need to let go."

"We're in a transition time. Not only is this our first year of marriage, but we're also finishing degrees, job searching, switching insurance companies, etc. We're learning to proactively communicate and take the time to sit down and talk, especially about finances. Blending our finances after getting married has been our greatest obstacle. During our first few years living together, we split everything 50/50, and didn't talk much about it, since we each had enough to pay the bills. We are getting better at more communication."

"Michael worked a long time to finish college. When I started my masters at a school in New Haven, Connecticut, Michael transferred so that we could support each other and commute together. This year, he finished his B.S. after eight years. He worked so hard, and I had never felt so proud of another person's success than when he walked across the stage at his graduation. He felt the same when I finished my M.S. a few months later. We worked as a team, and we did it together."

"It is a humbling feeling to belong to someone. We are very happy to have each other and to have made it official through marriage. We like the acceptance we receive from our international family. Now that we're married, we've become official members of each other's families."

"I just feel like getting married was saying officially to the world… 'alright we're together until we're dead.'"

"An amazing marriage to us is simple."

MELANIE *and* MARK

MARRIED 25 YEARS
HOCKESSIN, DELAWARE

"Mark and I met at a corporate safety fair. At the time, I was a single mother with two daughters, and my mother had invited us to attend. My mom introduced me to Mark. He was really sweet and attractive, but I wasn't interested. Due to difficult times in my life, I had no need or time to have anyone else in my life."

After persistently asking Melanie to join him for dinner, Mark was turned down, not once, but twice.

"About three weeks later, I was talking to my mom and she was telling me that Mark had asked how the girls and I were doing. After some encouragement from her, I broke down and called Mark to take him up on that dinner."

After a year of dating, they decided to get married and become a family unit.

Both coming from a marriage that had failed previously, they chose to take what they learned from those experiences and make sure their marriage did work.

"I had raised my daughters to believe they could do anything on their own. A man is a plus. I wanted them to know that Barbie doesn't need Ken. Barbie can be Barbie. She can fly an airplane. She can be an engineer. She can do whatever she wants to do. And if she wants, she can have the added benefit of being with a

friend, but she doesn't have to."

"I was very guarded. I think that is why Mark and I's marriage works. I know who I am, and I can do what I need to do, and how I need to do it. I have the benefit of having a wonderful husband, but we are here together because we want to be. We do things in partnership because we want to do it that way. We do this because this is who we are and who we want to be."

Before stepping into their marriage, they came up with an analogy about their lives that they often refer to. "I was on my island and he was on his. We decided that in order to make a bond, we had to jump off our islands to a new island, or it wasn't going to work. We have used that analogy for 25 years. I am an individual running our household. He is an individual running his career. Sometimes, it is easy to withdraw and go back to our islands. When that happens, we have to regroup and say, 'no, we are together, and we do this as a team.'"

One of Melanie and Mark's greatest challenges is Mark's career and his demanding global travel schedule that regularly takes him away from home for over half of the year. "There were many times I was exhausted and angry. But, I also respect him enough to know that is what provides for our family, and that is what makes him who he is. I didn't fall in love with someone who stays home every week. This has always been a part of who he is. I made that commitment to him. I made that commitment to my children, and that is who I am."

"We have learned over the years that you have to have a friendship and mutual respect for one another. We are not going to be the same; we are not going to think the same; we are not going to feel the same; but we have to respect each other's feelings. We have to have a friendship that can work its way through the challenges. It's like any relationship. You have to invest in it. When things are difficult, we have to invest time to get off our individual island and get back onto our island together."

"Our secret for a happy marriage is staying connected no matter the circumstances. Talk, touch, smile, and make each other and our family the most important thing in our lives. We must be willing to make the sacrifices that need to be made for the good of our relationship and family!"

"An amazing marriage is being married to my best friend. All of the other stuff is just added benefit. It does not mean that we spend every day and night together, but that we are molded together in our hearts. We are a team and a partnership that works in parallel. When we get to be together, it is the best!" ♥

RAE *and* WES

MARRIED 14 YEARS
MIRAMAR BEACH, FLORIDA

"A really exciting day for us came in December, 2014. It was the Monday after Christmas, and we sold our house. It was the house we had originally built to raise our children in and retire in. It was a bittersweet day. The exciting part started that night, when we officially moved into our RV full-time and moved to the beach. We absolutely love our life right now and haven't looked back for one second. We will eventually get another house, but right now, we are having a fun ride!" ♥

JEN and RYAN

MARRIED 11 YEARS
BROOKSVILLE, FLORIDA

Jen and Ryan met on the last day of their sophomore year of high school. Although Ryan "stood out as being crazy and one of the cool guys with his spiky tennis ball colored hair," it wasn't until their junior year that they really started to get to know one another while scooping frozen lemonade at an amusement park.

During the summer after their junior year, Ryan and Jen volunteered to take Ryan's little sister to an 'N Sync concert because his parent's original plans to take her had fallen through. As punk rock fans, they weren't really excited about 'N Sync. But it was during the concert that Ryan asked Jen to be his girlfriend.

They dated for four months and then broke up, because things got busy during their senior year and they drifted apart. Jen broke up with Ryan. "I was sad. That was the first time that I ever felt sad after breaking up with someone. That is when I knew our relationship was different."

Eventually they started talking again and hanging out more often. By February of their senior year, they were dating again.

"*If we wouldn't have broken up then, I don't think that we would have actually gotten married. We knew the second time that we got together that things were different. We learned through that hurt and breakup that the extent at which we did care for each other was more than we had initially thought.*"

On Ryan's 21st birthday, he proposed to Jen in New York City. They were married in Jen's backyard, in California, surrounded by 150 of their closest friends and family.

Jen grew up in a household where her parents taught her to be independent. They taught her that she could do everything and anything on her own. "Going into marriage, I stepped in thinking I would just handle everything. Over time with having kids, moving, having jobs, and just living life, it came to a place where I just realized it's not even fun thinking I can do it alone. It is really better when I invite Ryan into help me. Doing it alone, even if I was capable, isn't the way to go. Having us both involved in everything has helped me realize that it is better when we share responsibility."

"We came from families with very different views on money. The first year of marriage was a struggle, because the way we did finances was so different. That was a challenge for us at the beginning of our relationship."

"*Jen helped me to save money and get out of debt. Those two skills are so important to have in a marriage and to have less stress in life.*"

A few years into their marriage, Jen and Ryan bought a house in a town close to Jen's family. They had two children, Jackson and Clare. Ryan was commuting an hour to and from work, while

Jen was home taking care of their baby and two-year-old. "We were in very different roles. Ryan was working, and I was home with the kids. We didn't really talk. We lived in that house for a year and we did not have sex once in that house. I blocked that year out of my life. We were disconnected."

Jen was always exhausted after being home caring for the kids, and Ryan often felt frustrated. "*Jen is the only person I can be intimate with. There are not a whole lot of things in life that I can only do with her. It is exclusive. So, when she doesn't want to have sex and she is the only one that I can be intimate with, that is a recipe for frustration for both people. If you don't do it, you feel bad. And if you do do it, you still feel bad. It was a lose lose situation for us at the time.*"

"When Clare turned one, I remember having a realization where I thought, 'I think I am happy.'

But I didn't know, at the time, I wasn't happy. It was a really hard year, and we were both in survival mode."

The following year, they acted on an idea to

move to Florida to help plant a church. "The day we left felt so good. We were really aligned at this point. It felt like we were actually doing what we were supposed to do together. I feel like that is when things started to change for us. In Florida, we were able to spend so much more time together. It is what we needed to recover from that past year."

"Moving to Florida instantly shifted how we saw life. It became so unpredictable because there was no stability. Our mantra became, we have to plan on the unexpected happening. As we drove across the country from California to Florida, we didn't even know where we would land. With a three-year-old and a one-year-old, we didn't know where we were going to live. With finances, everything that I had thought would happen, didn't, and we were still okay. I had to let go of how my whole life was hardwired."

"My security shifted from us to other people. We know so many people that will help if we need it. Even if we don't know people, there are so many good people in the world that will help that I don't think we have to be so self-reliant anymore. That is why we have become so much more generous, too. Instead of hoarding everything that we make, we share it with others. There is more freedom in that."

"When things got really hard financially in Florida, I carried the burden of finding a way to make it work. Ryan never put that on me. I just always try to fix things. So, I just kept working. Simple Green Smoothies came out of that. Ryan supported that."

"When Jen does something, she does not mess around. I saw how hard she worked in school. There was never a doubt in my mind of 'is this going to work.'"

"Trust. That's a foundational thing for us."

"Marriage is hard, but really good. We have learned that it is important to be creative with how things can look. It is not always black or white. We are really good at seeing other ways to do things that are not expected or normal. It has given us opportunities to grow in different ways. We have fun outside of the norm."

"An amazing marriage is raising a family with someone you love." ♥

"Marriage is hard, but really good. We have learned that it is important to be creative with how things can look. It is not always black or white."

LAUREL *and* MICHAEL

MARRIED 5 YEARS
PENSACOLA, FLORIDA

"One of the things our pastor recommends is asking ourselves 'What is the next right thing?' Then, he says, 'Just do the next right thing.' Don't worry about tomorrow's decisions. What's the next right thing I can do today? Does my wife need me to unload the dishwasher? Do the next right thing. Does my son need me to hold him accountable and discipline him? Do the next right thing. I love that concept, because it just makes life a little simpler. That's really what we try to do… just be simple, without complicating things." ♥

OCTAVIA *and* DERRICK

MARRIED 13 YEARS
JONESBORO, GEORGIA

Octavia grew up on the West Side of Atlanta. At the age of nine, her 26-year-old mom passed away, her dad became a crack addict, and she took on the responsibility of her four younger siblings. She went to live with her grandparents, eventually 'spiraled out of control,' and was forced out of their home.

"When I was 12 years old, I met this guy who was 18 years old. He started taking advantage of me. He was sleeping with me, fighting on me, and beating me. I was a baby going through domestic violence. I made a lot of bad decisions and ended up running from foster home to foster home."

Derrick grew up on the South Side of Atlanta with only his mom present in his life. His mom moved to Savannah when he was 15 years old, and left Derrick in Atlanta to finish school.

"I was walking around the mall with one of my older friends when I spotted him. He didn't give me the time of day. I had to chase him. I was used to dating older guys. I didn't date people without cars or without being a drug dealer. I wanted the drug dealer, because the drug dealer could give me all of the material things. I needed someone who could help me help myself. But, Derrick was different. I just liked him."

"*I wasn't going to give her the time of day, but she pursued me. We were just friends who were kickin' it, having sex casually. We were not a couple.*"

Octavia and Derrick had their first child in 1996, when they were 15 and 16 years old. Their second child came shortly after. They were living separately and didn't actually become a couple until 1998.

"*In the beginning of our relationship, we did everything together. We sold drugs together; we went to the strip club together; we hung out and did everything together.*"

"People in our community didn't look up to the doctors or lawyers. We looked up to the dope dealers, because that is all we knew. We were making all kinds of money selling drugs and living recklessly. No one told us about saving money or credit."

"*The house we were staying in was the house we were selling drugs out of. One night, the police came, kicked the door in, and flooded the house. I claimed all the dope and was arrested.*"

"The best thing that happened to us was having the house busted. I truly thank God for my life and everything we have been through. When we tell people our story, it is hard for people to believe. God is a deliverer. You can make it. You can do it. You just have to want better. You have to get fed up with your situation. You have to take the cards that you were dealt and make the best hand possible."

"*I stopped selling drugs and got my first job making $10/hour. It was hard to go from making that much money, that fast, to go work a job making $10/hour. We were accustomed to a certain lifestyle. We didn't respect the money we had when we were dealing drugs. When we stopped selling, we had to reprogram ourselves and learn how to manage money. It was a struggle because we didn't know how to do that. However, it was worth it. I don't even miss the money. We actually have more than we ever had by not selling drugs. We have peace. We don't have to worry about going to jail. I don't have to worry about anybody kicking our door down. I have peace.*"

Octavia and Derrick were married May 26, 2001. "*When we were first married, we didn't know what to do.*"

"You don't know love until you have experienced love. Because I was so hooked up on the drug dealer, I almost lost my opportunity to experience true love that cannot be defined by anything material on this earth. Since we have been a part of a broken lifestyle all of our lives, it was hard to give each other that certain kind of love. I had to learn how to be a wife and how to be a lady, because I am from the hood. Even though I didn't know how to respond to love at the time, Derrick walked into my life, I am so glad that he stayed. I am so glad that he clearly could see something in me, that at the time I couldn't see in myself."

"*God allowed things to happen for us to grow and develop. When we had a house fire and lost everything, God allowed that to happen because He wanted to stir some things up in us.*"

"We knew we loved God. We knew we loved each other. However, it wasn't until we made God the foundation of our marriage that our relationship became stable."

"We believe that Jesus has to be the foundation. We believe that we have got to keep doors closed and can't give the Devil the opportunity to destroy our marriage. We had to grow up. We gotta be mature in our relationship. We have gotta be mature enough to know if we are being a jerk in our relationship, we must apologize. If my spouse keeps saying the same thing about me over and over again, I need to change it. If I cannot change it, I need to submit to God, and allow him to renew my mind, so that He can change me to better our relationship. We had to stop with the foolishness; stop with the façade; stop buying each other all these nice things when we are not giving each other all that we need outside of the material. We believe God will give us the balance to give each other everything that we want and need. But first and foremost, we need each other to be the man/woman of God that we were called to be, so that we can love each other properly."

Octavia and Derrick now have six children and are using their blessings to minister to the community where they were once arrested for dealing drugs.

"The things I was supposed to know as a father, I didn't know because I didn't have a father figure in my life. I knew I wanted to raise my kids. I wanted to be in the same household as my kids. I wanted to teach my kids, and instill things in them, that I didn't have growing up. We try to instill

values and integrity in them. We try to practice what we preach. We try as best we can to just make sure we live a good example and show our kids the dos and the don'ts in marriage."

"We are in a better place than we have ever been before. I am so excited that I get to do all of this life with my best friend, my husband."

"Since we have been together, everything we do is together. If we lose, we lose together. If we win, we win together. We come together as a team. That is how our marriage grows. A marriage is supposed to eliminate weaknesses. The areas where we were once weak when we were single, we are now strong. We complete each other. We complement each other. With Christ, we are whole together."

"An amazing marriage is not a perfect marriage, but a marriage that has been perfected through the eyes of God. It is one that can stand firm and stand united after weathering the storm." ♥

" An amazing marriage to us
is not a perfect marriage,
but a marriage that has been
perfected through the eyes of God.
It is one that can stand firm
and stand united after
weathering the storm. "

LINDSAY *and* KELI'I

MARRIED 15 YEARS
HAUULA, HAWAII

Lindsay and Keli'i grew up knowing one another because their dads are best friends. "I remember seeing Keli'i for the first time in a long time at a beach potluck party. I was 13 years old and he was 17 years old. I was old enough to realize that I could like older boys. I immediately decided that I was over the crush I had on Keli'i's little brother, and developed a huge crush on Keli'i."

At the time, Keli'i was living in Hawaii and Lindsay was living in Utah.

"I dated different guys in high school and Keli'i dated other girls as well, but I couldn't help but always wonder if something could come of us together. It wasn't until he returned home from his two-year church mission to Scotland, at age 21, and decided to go to college in Provo, Utah, that he was back in the picture for me. He came to Provo and my family was one of the only families he knew there. Within a couple months, we went from flirting to dating."

"We knew almost instantly, within two weeks of dating, that we would end up marrying each other. But we also knew that everybody in my family would be concerned because I was so young. So, to placate the family, we dated for another year and were engaged for about six months before we were married in July, 2000. I was 19 years old and Keli'i was 23 years old."

They moved into married student housing.

Three years later, they graduated from college and faced their first challenges together. Lindsay was pregnant with their first child, they moved to Hawaii, both started full-time jobs, and moved in with their parents to try to save money to buy a home. They quickly realized the "outrageous" cost of living in Hawaii. "It was a huge transition for both of us. It was definitely a time where we had to realign our goals and ambitions to work things out together for what we both wanted. We agree we came out of that experience much more unified and stronger together."

"We believe in eternal families and families that will be together forever. With that perspective, anything that comes up as a trial in our lives, we're able to work through together. It is just a small moment in the very big eternal picture for us as a family. The eternal goal gives us something to aim for when we face the bumps along the way."

Shortly after that year of transition, Lindsay and Keli'i moved back to Utah, where they had four more children within seven years.

In 2010, after a family road trip to Washington and Oregon, Keli'i suffered an unexpected and serious lung infection that collapsed his lung and required emergency surgery.

"While Keli'i lay sick, he frantically scribbled down all of our accounts and passwords for insurance info, etc. He honestly didn't know if he'd pull through and wanted to leave me with access to everything. It was definitely a very scary and sobering experience for us. We had four little kids at that time, ages two, four, five and seven. That was definitely a time where I felt like I could just fall apart."

"I remember talking to my dad at the time and he said, 'You are going to have to get through this. Everyone has to get through things that come their way. There is no way around it, but to go through and endure. To endure is a must, but to endure well is a choice.' For me, that's when I had a moment where I realized I needed to take this on with an attitude knowing we would get through. Because of our eternal perspective, I felt like we had a long way to go together. We were going to get through this."

Keli'i recovered 20 pounds lighter and very frail. He had months of healing and recovery.

"I would say that was one of the most significant and eye-opening experiences we've had in our marriage. I became very clear about my relationship with God, and with my husband. We realized just how fragile life is and how important our time is together."

In 2012, with a desire to raise their children closer to family, they moved back to Hawaii.

"We would definitely say the most exciting thing we've experienced together is parenthood. It's been a wild ride, especially having five kids within eight years, but it is by far the most rewarding thing we've experienced. One day our kids will marry and move out, and I want our marriage to be so strong when that happens. We will still have each other. Because of this, we make it a priority to go out on dates and enjoy spending time alone together. We want our kids to witness that, and be able to establish healthy, well-rounded relationships, later in their own life and within their own marriage."

"We've learned not to take our time together for granted, and to cherish one another. We find the most joy in serving one another selflessly,

and we believe that we are both complete and content, because we both give wholeheartedly to each other without question. We have our faith in God, our commitment to each other, our absolute loyalty and trust with each other, our service to one another, our friendship, our sense of humor and ability to laugh together, our communication, and our willingness to forgive and love unconditionally. It all works together to make a happy marriage."

"Love is a verb. It is an action. It is something we choose to do every day. It is always a work in progress, but it is always something that we choose to do."

"An amazing marriage to us is our marriage. We do everything in our power to fulfill each other's dreams and ambitions. We seek and give balance to one another, honesty, loyalty, a mutual respect for one another, genuine friendship, gratitude, compassion, laughter, love... I could go on. Our marriage really is an amazing marriage. We have something special and we don't take that for granted." ♥

"Love is a verb. It is an action. It is something we choose to do every day. It is always a work in progress, but it is always something that we choose to do."

RENEE *and* REESE

MARRIED 1 YEAR
HAUULA, HAWAII

"An amazing marriage is one that helps others see marriage as something to be cherished. We hear it over and over again, 'Marriage is hard work!' And that's true. It's sacrifice; it's forgiveness; it's dirty laundry (literally and figuratively); it's hard days; and, yes, it's sometimes painful. But, it's also an incredible gift. It's togetherness, laughter, patience, and dreaming. It's knowing someone better than anyone else in the world and being there for them. At its very core, marriage is love." ♥

MARY *and* RON

MARRIED 16 YEARS
CALDWELL, IDAHO

"Spontaneity is key in our relationship. We are always coming up with fun new things to do together. One day Mary suggested we get tattoos. I didn't hesitate. And now I have Mary tattooed on my leg." ♥

SIGGI *and* MARTELLUS

MARRIED 4 YEARS
LONG GROVE, ILLINOIS

Siggi and Martellus met during Martellus' NFL rookie football season in Dallas, Texas. They were introduced by a mutual friend at a nightclub. "At this point, I didn't think much about him except 'Wow, this guy is really tall!'" Martellus invited Siggi to a party he was throwing the following night. "I didn't realize, until I got there, that the party was the annual Dallas Cowboy's Thanksgiving Day Game After Party and that Martellus himself had played in the game earlier that day. At that time in my life, I could care less about football."

Siggi and Martellus casually continued their friendship via text while Siggi was away at Sarah Lawrence College in New York.

"Once I came back to Dallas on Christmas break, we began randomly running into each other, but I was a little weary of getting involved with a 'ballplayer.' One night, I ran into him at another nightclub. The second I walked off the elevator with my girls, I spotted tall, towering, Martellus standing in the middle of a group of women all fawning over him. He seemed to be enjoying the attention. But, the second he saw me walk off the elevator, and we caught each other's eye, the biggest grin cracked across his face."

"I began to walk toward him and I remember him reaching his arm over a few girls to grab my hand. He pulled me close to him and gave me the biggest hug and said, 'I'm so happy

you're here!' That was the moment I remember thinking, 'maybe I should give this guy a chance after all.'"

"There is something about Martellus' kid-like nature that drew me in. For me it wasn't a sense of immaturity, like it may have come off to some people. It was pure fun, a sort of innocence, and lack of seriousness, that I had been so accustomed to experiencing in my own life, but lacked over the last year since my father had passed. Martellus taught me how to relax again."

Siggi and Martellus casually dated more than two years until Siggi graduated from school. "I remember thinking how happy I was to have reached that point and to have accomplished my goal, but how sad I was that Martellus wasn't there to see me walk across the stage."

Siggi returned to Dallas after graduating and their relationship continued on and off. After a few weeks of not talking, Siggi received a message from Martellus saying he would leave her, and her family, tickets at Will Call for the Thanksgiving Day Football Game.

"During the game, I looked up to the exact spot in the stands where her seat would've been. I saw everyone there, my family and my friends, everyone except the person I wanted there most. In that moment, I realized that I never wanted to come out of the locker room after a home game

and not see Siggi's face smiling at me. Never again."

Four months later, Martellus proposed. Almost three months after that, Siggi and Martellus woke up one day and decided to skip the wedding planning and go to the Courthouse. Martellus wore a brown suit, and Siggi wore a blue dress. No one was there to witness, except Martellus' best friend, Dessie. "We got a lot of flack for that from our families who felt like we cheated them out of a very special moment. But, to this day, we don't regret it. It was the happiest day. It was our day, and it was perfect."

"From the beginning, Siggi was one of the most beautiful people I have ever seen in my life. She is the only person I have ever loved more than I love myself. When your significant other becomes your why, than everything is bigger than you."

Siggi and Martellus welcomed their daughter, Jett, about two years into their marriage.

"Having kids definitely helped me appreciate the little things in life and work harder to be the best version of myself. My whole goal is to be the man that I would want my daughter to marry. Whether it's as a father, or the way I treat her mom, I want her to see how much fun you can have in a relationship. I want her to grow up in an environment where we have breakfast for dinner, or dessert before dinner."

"It's nice to be a positive image of what love is suppose to be: treating each other as equals, respecting each other, and understanding that maybe there is a different perspective. I may not always agree with Martellus, but I can at least identify where he is coming from and respect that."

"Our best advice for couples is to never stop growing. As individuals as well as a unit, constant evolution is key. When we are complacent, that's when things become stagnant. I think a lot of times people get lost in each other's identities. There is always an 'us,' but there should always be a 'you' and an 'I,' because that is what makes us 'us.' When people experience growth separately, it isn't natural. Take a tree for example. If a branch has outgrown the trunk, that branch falls off the trunk, although that trunk is still the same. If it grows together at the same time, then the tree will always stay intact."

"Martellus and I are polar opposites. His head is always going, going, going. He has so many things that he is passionate about. It is so cool to watch, but can be intimidating at times. He is not afraid to fail. He says, 'well, just try it. You might love it. Sometimes you don't succeed, but at least you tried.'"

"I kind of fade to the background most of the time. That's been a challenge of ours. He's always pushing me to not give up on things that I want to do, because I am so enthralled in family life. To be Jett's caretaker is my passion. Martellus is always saying, 'No, you still have other dreams that you have to keep pursuing. You can't just spend your whole day with your life revolving around us all of the time.'"

"Although challenging, that is also one of the best things about being married, 'the feeling of always having someone in my corner to be my biggest fan, to challenge me, to push me to be my best, and protect me.'"

"An amazing marriage is being with someone who doesn't always pick your weeds, but waters your plants." ♥

CHRISTY *and* JAMES

MARRIED 6 YEARS
CHICAGO, ILLINOIS

"Although running a business together and keeping it thriving has most definitely been a challenge in and of itself, the most difficult thing we've been through together is battling infertility. We tried for four years (off & on), before we finally gave in to the fact that there may be an issue, and we should probably see a specialist. In 2013, we finally took steps to move forward with a fertility doctor. In 2014, we went through three failed IUIs, which was exhausting, expensive, and emotionally heartbreaking for us. We learned so much about each other and our marriage through the process, and it made us even closer and more grateful for what we do have. In 2015, we went through two rounds of IVF. The first round resulted in a miscarriage, which was one of the most difficult things we've ever been through. The second round was finally successful and we are now expecting twin boys. We are actually so grateful to have been down this road together and know we are right where we are meant to be now." ♥

CARLY *and* BOBBY

MARRIED 3 YEARS
INDIANAPOLIS, INDIANA

"Bobby and I met in Fall, 2006 at Miami University, in Ohio. He was a junior, and I was starting the first year of my master's program. I was the advisor to AfterDark, a student programming board, and he was a member. We quickly became friends, bonding over our shared love of the show *24*. We were friends that whole year, both while dating other people. Bobby left for the summer to do an internship in Washington, D.C. We stayed in touch and talked on the phone. When school started again in August, we picked up right where we left off. I think we both realized we had missed each other. By late fall, we had ended our relationships with other people, and went on our first date. The tricky thing was, since I was a grad student and he was an undergrad, we weren't supposed to be dating. So,

we basically had a secret relationship for the whole spring semester."

After graduation, Bobby already had a job lined up back in his hometown in Indianapolis. "I'm originally from the East Coast, but I decided to take a chance on our relationship and also took a job in Indiana. We lived about 90 minutes apart for two years. Then, in the Fall of 2010, we moved in together, and he proposed in October."

Carly and Bobby were married in August, 2011, bought a house in Indianapolis in 2012, and welcomed their son, Jack, in the Spring of 2014.

"We both come from great close families. So, we knew we wanted to have kids, and we had talked about that. We were both on the same page and excited to start a family."

"Nothing beats the end-to-end journey of having a kid. From the very beginning, when we discussed if we were ready to try, to the moment Jack was born, it was an unbelievably fun, challenging, and exciting adventure. And it hasn't stopped since."

"Having a baby is a blessing, but it totally changed our life and marriage. I always heard people say that the first year of marriage is the hardest, but I think that was a breeze compared to the first year of parenthood. All of a sudden, our life was totally consumed with this new baby. It's easy to forget that before we were parents, we were individuals, and also a couple."

"We have learned that it is important to support each other's individual interests and activities. We think it's important to have our own identity outside of our marriage, in addition to having a strong partnership. For example, Bobby goes to Colts and Pacers games, and I workout a few times a week, or have a wine night with friends. Obviously, we love spending time together, but we don't get all of our fulfillment just from each other."

Although new parenthood was tough on their relationship, Carly and Bobby said it helped them recommit to their partnership. "We really had to rely on each other, communicate clearly about our needs, and give each other grace and forgiveness. Having a baby forced us to be on the same page and be more aware when the other person needed help. It forced us to communicate non-stop. Now we have an extra level of being considerate of each other's needs. Overall, being parents has made us appreciate everything that the other person does and makes us want to help in return."

"Our everyday life involves a lot of teamwork and dividing and conquering. We're very equal as far as our household and parenting duties. It's just nice to have a partner at all times, to know we have someone to wake up next to, and to have coffee with in the morning. We love having a teammate in everything that we do. It is very comforting. Having a built in sounding block and someone to bounce ideas off of, seek advice, and discuss personal and professional goals, is something we love about being married."

"It is so great to have a person who challenges me and helps me be a better person and a better parent. Parenthood is a crazy journey and I am glad I have someone to do it with. It's more fun to go through it with someone else."

"An amazing marriage is finding that someone who lets you be 100% authentic and loves you for it." ♥

LISA *and* JOEL

MARRIED 10 YEARS
CLIVE, IOWA

Lisa and Joel met on a blind date, set up by mutual friends, while both attending Graduate School at Iowa State University. "*I had never really been on a blind date before. I just remember thinking 'please be cute.' I kept saying that over and over in my head as I walked up to the door 'Please be cute. Please be cute.' She opened the door and she was.*"

After their third date, Joel was sure Lisa was the one. "*I went back to my apartment and I told my roommate that I was 99% certain that I was going to marry her.*" Lisa was less certain, but the fact that Joel could bake a mean cheesecake kept her hanging around for more. Joel proposed under the Campanile at Iowa State University seven months after their first date. They were married in October, 2004.

Lisa now stays at home with their three children, while Joel works. "I was a career woman climbing the professional ladder. Motherhood has been something I really struggle with. The first time we were pregnant, it was very early on in our marriage, and then we lost the baby to a miscarriage. That really put a lot of fear into me like 'what is wrong with me; will I have more miscarriages; is my fertility broken?' All of these fears flooded my mind and I didn't want to go through that again. I didn't want to go through the heartache of losing another baby."

"We did get pregnant again with Lucy. However,

Lucy was a twin, and we lost her sibling. Joel's reaction was 'holy crap, we are one for three. How can we be that bad at this?' It was a hard balance trying to be happy because we had a healthy baby, but we knew she had a twin. We struggled to figure out how to deal with that whole dynamic."

When Lucy was about a year old, Lisa's father tragically died. "That was a real turning point for me. I kept asking myself, 'if I died tomorrow like my dad did, what would be my biggest regret?' My answer was 'denying Joel his wife, Lucy her mom, and me an opportunity to fulfill those roles.' So I had a '*Forrest Gump* moment' and quit running the race, in order to come home and be with our kids."

Lisa and Joel handled the loss of Lisa's father and their babies very differently. "*When you consider the fact that it was my father-in-law, despite how close I was to him, it wasn't my father. With the miscarriage, it was my child, but it wasn't my body. For both of those tragedies, I was standing on the sidelines trying to figure out how I could help. I learned to be patient. There is this thing called the Ministry of Presence, just being there and being available. I think as men we struggle with, 'how can I get in and fix this. What can I do?' Sometimes the thing that we should do is just be there and be patient, ask a question every now and then, and just be available, because that's what is needed. There are things that you can't just pick up a wrench and fix somehow. That is the truth in a lot of things in marriage."*

Lisa's job was social. She was in the public eye and constantly around people. "I went from that, to being home with small children. I lost my social circle; I lost conversation; I lost a reason to get up and take a shower. I was very lazy. I continuously prayed desperately for the grace to love my family, my husband, and my children like Jesus loves me. It's happening. It's slowly being revealed, 'This is how you do it.'"

Lisa takes time on Saturday to restore and renew. "They are my 'Mother Sabbaths.' I take them as often as I can, even if it's just for an hour. Joel knows I need some woman-to-woman conversation to have my spiritual tank filled, in order to do life day in and day out. He has a phrase that we live by 'when nothing is in it for you, everything is in it for you.'"

"Being committed to our marriage, no matter how much it's ever cost me in any given moment, has brought me back more than I could ever have possibly imagined. The idea of getting out of our marriage couldn't be further from our consciousness. It's just not on our radar screen. Nothing about our marriage is optional. Everything about it is mandatory. And we embrace that and wouldn't have it any other way."

"Pray, work, rest, and play is our family motto, and we strive to live in a balance of those four virtues day in and out. We take joy in 'holy leisure' and wasting time with one another."

"Joel is my life's companion and that in itself is amazing. Knowing that I have somebody who I want to share every single part of my existence with is incredible. I don't want anybody else to be there for the milestones and even the mundane. Joel's there for the mundane and the exciting. There is no one else I'd rather journey through life by my side." ♥

ALEXANDRIA *and* TYLER

MARRIED 2 YEARS
AMES, IOWA

"Our relationship works because we put God at the center of our marriage and rely on him during the hard times. We also came into our marriage with an attitude that separation is not an option. It is hard work, and it is going to continue to be hard work for the rest of our lives. It takes effort." ♥

SHEFALI and BRYAN

MARRIED 4 YEARS
KANSAS CITY, KANSAS

Shefali and Bryan met in the Fall of 2003 at the University of Missouri-Rolla. Bryan was a junior and Shefali was a freshman, both were working towards engineering degrees.

"I wasn't really allowed to date in high school. Bryan was my first real boyfriend and my last one. We joked back then to our family and friends that we had found the 'girl' and 'boy' version of ourselves in the other."

"We faced a major challenge early in our relationship. My mom and dad had this idea that I would marry an Indian boy. My mom and dad were not happy at all. They didn't like that I was dating Bryan, a country boy. They thought that this was just a 'friend thing' that would eventually go away. They could not understand how we would make a relationship work being from two different religions and cultures."

Shefali's parents had an arranged marriage. They met, were engaged, and were married, all in the same week. "They never understood that you meet somebody and you fall in love. Bryan is my best friend, but he is also the guy I want to be with for the rest of my life."

In 2009, after five years of dating, Shefali lost her job and was diagnosed with celiac disease all within 24 hours. "I got really sick. My mom watched me throw up everywhere and she didn't know what to do. But, Bryan immediately knew

what to do. He pulled my hair back and rubbed my back. I think when my parents saw me fall, and they saw how much he took care of me, they didn't care about the cultural differences anymore. Ever since that day, I have never gone a day without hearing how great of a guy Bryan is, and how much they love him."

"It was really hard for my parents to see past color and religion. To them, they have only known the Indian culture. They never had friends who married outside of the culture. I was the first one to break that barrier."

Shefali and Bryan were married on June 19th, 2010. They mixed both Shefali's Indian culture and customs with Bryan's Irish and Catholic roots into their ceremony and reception. "It was amazing to watch our families come together from such different origins and have immense joy and love on their faces."

"Today, we have a healthy and rambunctious little man who surprises us with what he is learning daily. Having Noah has strengthened our marriage, and he is our daily reminder of dreaming big, loving life, and being so grateful for each day given to us. God is good, and He shows us every day, there will be challenges that will come our way, but if we communicate and stay strong together, we can overcome anything and show our children anything is possible."

"All of the challenges we have faced have taught us to embrace our future and be grateful for one another. We have learned that we have to make compromises if we want to make a marriage work. We were given the best advice when we were engaged. Someone told us to 'make sure you always put the other person first.' If you put the other person first and they put you first, then one of you will always have the other and be taken care of."

"Our favorite thing about being married is experiencing life, parenthood, and the world with our best friend. There is so much joy having someone by your side to celebrate all of life's moments and to care for in the way you want to be cared for. Marriage is a complete blessing, and we have learned to never take it for granted. Life is short, and we feel grateful to have found a life-long best friend to grow old and experience life with." ♥

"Marriage is a complete blessing, and we have learned to never take it for granted. Life is short, and we feel grateful to have found a life-long best friend to grow old and experience life with."

MELISSA *and* GARY

MARRIED 1 YEAR
LEXINGTON, KENTUCKY

Melissa and Gary went to the same high school and started to hang out with the same group of friends toward the end of their senior year. "This continued as we attended the University of Kentucky, but eventually, we started hanging out one-on-one. The week before finals during our fall semester, we stayed in the library one day until 6:00 a.m. just talking. We were young and in love and just wanted to soak it all in."

After dating for over two years, Gary proposed to Melissa. They received a lot of opposition from their families.

"*I just remember feeling like it was us against everyone. They didn't want us to get married so young. They wanted us to wait and have more money and degrees. From our point of view, there was no reason not to get married. I knew for a fact that I wanted to spend the rest of my life with Melissa. I knew that we were both mature enough, and she complemented me extremely well. Neither of our families really understood that, because they had a different perspective on marriage than we did. Their view of marriage was very image based... a house, money, jobs, and all those things. Our view of marriage is two people saying I want to give my life for you, and I plan on doing that every day for the rest of my life. We don't care about money. We don't care about whatever career we choose. It's just a matter of us getting to be together and starting our lives together.*"

"We were 20 years old and engaged. Looking at it logically from their perspective, I can understand why they were concerned. However, we knew that we were going to get married on that day in January. It was just a matter of whether or not our family was going to be there. Eventually, they warmed up to it. We just had to be patient and graceful with them."

"We feel incredibly blessed to have found each other at such a young age, because we've both gotten to see each other grow and push each other to become the people the Lord has designed us to be."

Melissa and Gary were married on January 4, 2014, with their families in attendance, three years after they started dating.

"*Love is painted in such an emotional picture these days through the movies and T.V. shows. It's always so emotional. It's always 'I'm so physically attracted to you and emotionally in love with you.' Love is not emotionally based. It is something you have to choose. When I married Melissa, I had no idea what she was going to be like 20 years from now, or 30 years from now. Marriage is making a statement that I choose to love her no matter who she becomes and no matter what kind of sickness she endures. I promise to always choose to love Melissa.*"

"*When we were married I felt like I knew what*

it meant to give my life to someone. But, I don't think I truly understood the gravity of what giving grace to your spouse truly means. That's something I have had to learn as I do it."

"People are always going to fail. We are both fallen people and we are not perfect in any way. If we entered into marriage without a foundation built on something as wonderful and big and awesome as God, then we would have built our foundation on each other. If our foundation was built on each other, then the foundation would have crumbled because we are imperfect."

"*My expectations for marriage were very simple. You get a joint bank account. You sleep in the same bed. You get to have sex. And you wake up every day next to your best friend.*"

"I expected us to spend a lot of time together. I just expected us to always be together and always hanging out. While Gary was balancing being a full-time student and working part-time at Starbucks, we didn't seem to get as much quality time as we wanted. It was difficult because I was falling into the trap of comparison. Saying to myself, 'As newlyweds, I thought it would look more like them.' Or 'I don't see my husband as much as every other wife does.' Or 'Why can't we buy new decorations for our apartment and make it as cute as so-and-so's?' But, the Lord slowly changed my heart and made me more content with our situation. I learned to find joy in the things that we do have, instead of thinking about what we don't."

Over their first year of marriage, Melissa and Gary have implemented a lot of the advice they have received about marriage. "Put your spouse's needs before your own needs. Be as selfless as possible in all that you do. Humble yourself. Get good at forgiving each other early. Say sorry a lot. Never go to bed angry. Shower together to enjoy more quality time together."

"One of our favorite things to do together is go on walks with our sweet little dog. It's a great way to disconnect from the busy demands of life. It's where we just talk about our dreams, fears, worries, and everything. I love doing life with my best friend, the one person that understands me the most." ♥

"When I married Melissa, I had no idea what she was going to be like 20 years from now, or 30 years from now. Marriage is making a statement that I choose to love her no matter who she becomes and no matter what kind of sickness she endures. I promise to always choose to love Melissa."

BARBARA *and* BOB

MARRIED 36 YEARS
BENTON, LOUISIANA

Barbara and Bob met in college at Louisiana Tech in 1974. They were on a ski boat during a fraternity formal weekend. "We fell in lust. I was in a bikini and he had on really short cutoffs. To this day, he couldn't tell you what my face looked like."

However, their lust turned to love rather quickly. They met in April and had their first date in October. "We were inseparable by December and stayed that way for years."

Once Bob graduated from college, they were married and moved to New Orleans a few weeks after. Bob immediately started his first job as a Petroleum Engineer in the oil and gas industry.

"The oil and gas industry through its history, has been very volatile. There are periods of extreme prosperity and periods of staggering decline. We lived through several of the cycles and two of them ended up with layoffs. I was out of work twice. During the first layoff, I was out of work for 10 months. In that time, our son, our second child, was born with a birth defect. He spent two months in the neonatal intensive care unit. Without question, that was the most trying time that we've had together."

"The near death of our newborn son was a recalibrating event that forced us to really take a look at what's important. It brought us closer. We're a team. We are at opposite ends of the temperament spectrum, but we're a team. During the years that were lean financially, he went out and did his part by trying to find as much work as he could. I did my part by stretching a dollar as far as I could. I didn't think our money problems were his fault, and he didn't think they were my fault. It was a thing we were in together. It was part of the playbook for our team."

"Due to Bob's work, I used to joke and tell people I was a married single parent raising three children. It was hard to not be together for long stretches while he traveled. I think we fell so deeply in love early on, that during the times when that would wane, it was still the anchor to our relationship. Divorce was never an option. There was no divorce in my family going back generations. It just wasn't in our family vocabulary."

"I have a belief that you will fall in and out of love your whole life."

"I think it's more you fall in and out of like. The love is there, but there's certain periods of time when you just really don't care for each other that much. It's not all wine and roses. We have had whole periods of time where we didn't like each other very well, but we knew we still loved each other."

"Mary Chapin Carpenter has a song that says 'we got this far, darling, not by luck, but by never turning back.' That's what you do. You stick to it and do whatever it takes. You have to make yourself happy. Bob can't make me happy. I can't make him happy."

"*It's very difficult to 'have it all'... to have a big successful professional career, a successful family, successful children, and all of that kind of stuff. Balancing all of that stuff was just unbelievably hard. I think it's especially hard for one person to balance all of those things. It takes a team to be able to do that. So, if somebody is pulling on this rope when I don't have the ability or the strength to pull on that rope, Barbara is pulling on that rope for me.*"

A few years ago, after many years of living hundreds of miles from work and waking up every Monday morning at 3:00 a.m. to travel for the week, Barbara and Bob decided to make a change. "*It got really frustrating that I'd be sitting on the couch watching a T.V. show, she'd be sitting on the couch watching a T.V. show, we'd be playing 'Words with Friends,' and texting back and forth, because the couches were 170 miles apart. At that moment, we thought, 'you know, maybe we'd like to try to live together before we die.'*" Of course, then that presented the question, '*Can we live together?' I mean I tell people, we've been married for 37 years. We've* lived together for 20 of those years and they've been 10 of the happiest years of our lives.*"

Barbara and Bob are "finally" living together full-time. "We live on a beautiful lake and travel often."

"Our marriage is amazing because after nearly 37 years of marriage, and 40 years together, we still make each other laugh and still have fun together." ♥

JONI *and* TORI

MARRIED 12 YEARS
INDUSTRY, MAINE

Joni and Tory met in seventh grade when Joni's family moved into town. They shared the same one hour bus ride to and from school. They started going out in eighth grade and stuck together from that point on. "We just became an institution, and no one expected anything different of us. We were named 'class couple' our senior year of high school."

After graduating from high school, Tory went on a road trip with his friend across the country. "*We thought we would be out longer, but it only took a month to realize where I wanted to be.*" Tory surprised Joni back in Maine just a few weeks after he left.

Tory moved in with Joni and eventually, they moved to a cabin in the woods behind Tory's parent's home. "*It didn't have any running water. It was such a cozy spot. I would heat up water and put it in a black sled, next to the wood stove, to heat up so Joni could take her bath. Life was so simple then. We lived there for a couple of years. Those are the best memories.*"

About one year after getting engaged, they were married at 20 years old.

"Our wedding was epic. I think we spent a total of $1500 on the entire wedding. We were married in my parent's backyard and then had a reception about four miles away at Tory's parent's house. People still talk about the party!"

"*At the time of getting married, we were still living in the woods and loving it. However, we have always had ongoing house plans. I've always said, 'our plans can change daily, but if we don't have a goal that we are working towards, then we are not headed for anything.'*"

"We were really young when we bought our first house. It was the house I grew up in and the house where we were married. We moved out of our cabin. Tory was self-employed and I was a nanny. The only way we could pay the mortgage was by renting out the second floor apartments. It was always a struggle. A few years ago, after a series of unfortunate rental unit situations, we had to let go of our house through a foreclosure process. It was a scary time, but we had faith. Somehow, through a bunch of tiny and big miracles, we came through it. Tory was my rock throughout the process and continues to be. Now, we are settled in a little log cabin in the woods. We have always been and continue to be down to earth people, focused on the important stuff in life. We try not to worry about the fluff."

"We are pretty excited to be raising two really cool kids. We homeschool them, so we spend a lot of time together. They make us laugh, and they make us nutty. There's never a dull moment."

"It was really hard to have kids so young. We were 21 years old and I don't think we knew how hard it was going to be. It definitely changed our identity. From the moment we got home from the hospital, I remember thinking, 'Whoa. This is real. Zinnia is real and she is really our daughter.' It changed my identity a lot and it still does. Being a homeschool mom is a huge part of my identity too. There is so much pressure, and I constantly feel like I am failing most of the time. But I know it is only for a season. Our kids are going to grow up and we are still going to be pretty young."

"It's really easy when married to forget that your spouse is not just an extension of you. It is so important to remember he/she is another human who deserves to be treated with kindness and respect. Take each other seriously and be kind, flexible, generous, and understanding. Randomly bringing home chocolate is always a good idea too."

"I really love Tory. We are best friends. We grew up together. Usually we are right on the same page about everything. We are so grateful to have each other as a partner in all of our life adventures."

"An amazing marriage is a marriage where you support each other's dreams, even the crazy ones." ♥

"An amazing marriage is
a marriage where you support
each other's dreams,
even the crazy ones."

AMY *and* GREG

MARRIED 34 YEARS
ANNAPOLIS, MARYLAND

"We first saw each other at Nield Street Deli at West Chester University in October of 1980. I lost a bet to pick up the hoagies, and he was there with his fraternity buddy picking up dinner. We made eye contact. It was just a glance."

"Within the next month, I went to a party at his fraternity. My friend was setting me up with another guy, so we went to the party at TKE. She left me and some 'twit' was bugging me when Greg approached me with his hand extended. He said, 'Hi, I'm Greg Barber, how do you like me so far?' I laughed and the 'twit' left. I thanked Greg for getting him away from me. We chatted, but then I met some other guys. A little while later, I started to date Greg's roommate, Dave. Eventually, there was a terrible triangle. Greg wanted me, Dave had me, and I was all flustered. The boys argued and I just kept quiet."

Greg won the battle and he took Amy to the Red Carnation Ball the next semester. Two years later, they walked down the aisle together with Dave as their groomsman and still their friend today.

"When you get married, you take vows. Those vows have meant a lot to us. For richer or poorer and in sickness and in health. They don't sound like much at first, but being married this long, we can contemplate. One may think 'in richness' has to do with money. It doesn't. Our life has been made so rich with our children. We have the most amazing children. I would say that they are the best of Greg and me, but they are so much more than us. I see a little of both of us in all of them. But, I see so much more too. They are achieving things that Greg and I always wanted to do but didn't have much guidance. We tried to be there all the time with that guidance for them. We have always been known as 'The Barbers.' You know, that healthy perfect family that excels in everything they do. So, that vow…'In health'… we had that conquered."

Then, at the age of 50, Amy found out by accident that she had Kidney Cancer. They removed a grapefruit sized tumor, but unfortunately, just two years later, the cancer came back. She now has stage four cancer.

"Unfortunately, Kidney Cancer doesn't really go away and chemo and radiation doesn't help. But, we can extend my life with medications and occasional surgeries. Greg has been my rock."

"*My mom died of cancer when I was just nine years old. My dad was strong. I just watched him. He raised four kids after my mom died. He took care of everything. It's my responsibility. It's my end of the deal.*"

"It is so important to have a partner. We are just such good companions. Everything is not romantic and roses in your life. You have to be good companions."

"We have been through a lot of bumpy times. But we always go through them together. That stuff just makes us stronger."

After just three years of marriage, Amy and Greg were startled by the noise of a drug-induced man who broke into their home. Greg was a police officer at the time and actually recognized the criminal. After that traumatizing experience, Amy had a hard time sleeping and was scared often. "It was rough for quite a while. Then, Greg's fraternity brother offered him a job in Annapolis,

and we leaped. I didn't realize then how much Greg was giving up for our family. He loved being an officer, but our family was more important to him."

"*You can't plan on the future. We didn't plan on someone breaking into our home. I didn't plan on not being a cop.*"

"Our favorite thing about being married is that we get to go through everything together. I'm never alone and we are a stronger force together by being married."

"An amazing marriage is friendship that leads to companionship. It sounds boring when you are young, but when you have been together as long as us, you will understand the need to be companions." ♥

"We have been through
a lot of bumpy times.
But, we always go through
them together. That stuff
just makes us stronger."

ALLISON *and* TOM

MARRIED 13 YEARS
ANNAPOLIS, MARYLAND

"All of our obstacles seem crazy and unbelievable when we sit down and list them. But honestly, Tom and I have been really good about taking one thing at a time. There is no point in getting upset about the things we can't handle. We just have to do what we have to do today. We try not to pile on the bad and always try to focus on one thing that is good in every situation. We have perfected the art of making lemonade out of lemons. And, we laugh a lot...because if we didn't, we would cry...a lot."

"We are always in 'this' together. We are a team. We take turns being the strong one. We approach every win and loss with that same attitude. We don't point fingers and we don't keep score. We support each other, cheer for each other, and love each other. #TeamBarnhill is our motto and that is what gets us through the obstacles."

"An amazing marriage to us is teamwork." ♥

LINDSAY *and* JESSE

MARRIED 6 YEARS
AMESBURY, MASSACHUSETTS

"We met in high school. I was a junior and Jesse was a senior. During his last week of school, he came up to my car and asked what I was doing after school. I (so appropriately) said 'you.' My best friend, Kaylin, and I hung out with Jesse that night. The next day Jesse broke up with his girlfriend he had at the time, and we've been together ever since."

Lindsay and Jesse dated for eight years before getting married. They dated long-distance for years, while Jesse owned his own business in Rhode Island and Lindsay went to school at the University of New Hampshire.

"*I knew before eight years of dating that I would marry her. But going through life events*

together… happy times and bad times… really allowed us to get to know each other and understand each other. We learned all of the weird things about each other and it made them more tolerable. Marriage is a big deal and it is okay to take that time. It takes a lot more than people think to go through life together."

"Both of our parents were divorced within the same year that we were married. Each situation was exactly the same, but we handled it very differently. We felt different things at the same time, but we could always respect the other person's feelings. Even though we had gone through the same thing, we had to realize that people deal with things differently. We developed an understanding for each person's highs and lows."

"While our parents were going through their divorces, we had a conversation about our marriage. We said, 'out of respect for one another, should anything happen, just come to each other first. Should something get to that bad of a place, instead of going outside of the marriage, let's just talk about it.' We made that agreement early on in our marriage."

"I remember the first year being tough. I would, or Jesse would, assume that we were hanging out without making plans. But we would never talk about it. We were coming from a long distance relationship where everything was planned. I think when we started living together, we just thought we didn't have to plan anymore.

That wasn't true. We had to communicate much more. That was hard for us and is still hard."

"The most exciting thing we have gone through together is the birth of our twin boys. We wanted kids, but one at a time. Having kids was not a surprise. Having twins was a surprise."

"We joked through our years together that Jesse would be a stay at home dad. When we had twins, it was the universe saying, okay this is going to happen." Jesse stays home with the boys while Lindsay works.

"We don't take ourselves too seriously. We are serious about the things that we need to be serious about."

"Our best advice for marriage is to make sure you take time for yourself. Don't lose your independent spirit. The more you know you can survive without each other, the better you survive together."

"Getting to hangout with my best friend everyday is the best thing about marriage. We still schedule time for just us, but coming home to the person that knows me best is wonderful. We don't get sick of each other. We fundamentally think the same way. We understand each other. We are friends."

"An amazing marriage is crazy, happy, complicated… and a little silly." ♥

"The more you know you can survive without each other, the better you survive together."

JOANN *and* SYL

MARRIED 44 YEARS
WASHINGTON, MICHIGAN

JoAnn and Syl met at the young age of 15. They went to the same grade school and lived down the street from one another. Syl came from a family of five boys and JoAnn came from a family of four girls. So naturally, they hung out in the neighborhood together.

"That summer was the best of my life." By the end of that summer, Syl asked JoAnn to go steady. "We knew almost instantly that we were meant to be together. And, once we were, that was it." They were married six years later.

"Being together for almost 50 years, a lot happens. You grow. I am not the person by any means that I was when we met at 15 years old. It takes a lot of commitment to go from 15 years old to 65 years old with one person, and to love them more now than when we first met. We formed a partnership. That's really what a marriage is. It is a partnership. It's not about who is in control, or who wins the arguments. It's about being partners, and that is what makes a marriage work."

"One of our biggest challenges in marriage that we faced is falling in and out of love with one another. Sometimes you just don't like each other anymore. After asking ourselves, 'Do I leave? Do I give up?' The answer was always 'No.' We learned to wait. And, after a bit, we saw it again: that smile, that spark, and that laughter. It comes back. And, we fall in love all over again. But, better and deeper."

"We will soon be embarking on the Fall season of our lives. Retirement is as difficult of a turn of events as getting married, or having children, or changing a job. It is a huge change. Those are the phases that will make or break you. I expect this season to be filled with things yet left undone: aspirations, hopes, and dreams to reach towards. This will be our time, a new beginning, with opportunities on the path ahead."

"Our best advice for other couples is to marry your best friend… someone you trust to lift you up when you are down. Someone who will support you in your choices, hear you out, and still walk with you even if they aren't fully on board, simply because you are passionate about your goal. Do the same for them. Laugh together. Hold hands. Respect each other and like him/her for who he/she is. Don't marry someone to fix them. Marry your best friend because you love that quirky thing they do!"

"*I would have to say having married my best friend is the best thing that has ever happened. I wouldn't have done it any other way with any other woman. I have just been the happiest, luckiest, man in the world.*"

"An amazing marriage is complete trust and unconditional love." ♥

ALEXANDRA *and* KURTIS

MARRIED 2 YEARS
CRYSTAL, MINNESOTA

Alexandra and Kurtis met during their first year of Law School. "Our second year, we joined a coed recreational soccer league and that is where the flirtation started. We began dating that year and at the end of school, we moved in together. We dated another year, and by then, we just knew that we wanted to spend our lives together."

There wasn't an engagement ring or a formal proposal for Alexandra and Kurtis. They just decided one day when coming home from a dinner with friends that they were going to get married.

"It was never about the wedding for us. A three-month engagement was followed by an intimate wedding at my family's lake home. We had a very small wedding. We cut out all of the frills that we possibly could because we always believe they take away from what is suppose to be the heart of the day. Our wedding was a reflection of who we are. We have never felt like we needed to have a big show of anything. I was most excited to make that commitment in front of friends, to say our vows, and to be Kurtis' wife. A wedding is just one day. It is a few hours of one day. Marriage is for 60+ years."

"I didn't have many expectations for marriage because I didn't think much would change. We had already been living together, we went through law school, and passed the bar together. I figured if we could do all of that together, we could probably have a pretty decent marriage."

Facing the start of their careers after Law School and studying for the Bar Exam together was a challenge. "The pressure was high and we each have such different studying styles. It was important to us to find a healthy outlet for our stress, so we decided to tackle a major landscape project at our house. It got us out of the house, away from the books, while still spending time together. It turned what could have been a horrible couple of months into a wonderful summer."

"*The beauty of falling in love when you are in school is knowing that school is always going to end. Change is going to come no matter what after that. I think we would be foolish to think we were going to be the same person in school and out of school. It is okay to change a little and give a little, understanding that 50 years from now I won't be the same person that Alex married and she won't be the same person that I married. We will grow together.*"

"I like to think that we are stronger together than we are apart. The longer we are together, the better our relationship will be."

"This year, our family of two will grow to a family of three. We are pumped to become parents and welcome a tiny human into our home. It's fun to see Kurtis transition into being a father. It's a different side of him I haven't seen before. We are entering the unknown right now. We are focused on becoming parents, but still want to keep our relationship first. It is fun, but scary at the same time."

"Marriage is one day at a time. There are going to be good days and bad days. We are lucky that we get to go to bed next to each other and wake up next to each other. At the end of the day, when we look at each other and say 'I love you,' it's pretty great."

"An amazing marriage is full of love, conflict, resolution, and happiness. ♥

"A wedding is just one day.
It is a few hours of one day.
Marriage is for 60+ years."

SARAH JOY *and* BRAD

MARRIED 1 YEAR
OXFORD, MISSISSIPPI

Sarah Joy and Brad met at a Jon Foreman concert in November of 2011. Sarah Joy's sister and Brad's brother were interested in each other and needed someone else to tag along with to the concert. They all had a great time and ended up being a group of friends that often hung out together. Sarah Joy's sister and Brad's brother went separate ways, but Sarah Joy and Brad stayed in touch and developed a strong friendship.

"*I remember telling my mom in the car one day without even really thinking much about it, 'You know, Sarah Joy is the kind of person that I should be trying to date.'*"

During the Summer of 2012, before Brad started Law School at Ole Miss, Sarah Joy invited Brad to her family reunion. She prepped her whole family ahead of time, so they knew they were "just friends." However, during a game of volleyball, Sarah's cousin, Chris, brought up dating. "*He looked over at me as I raised the beach ball and said, 'Okay Brad, this serve will be the test to determine whether you're worthy to date Sarah Joy or not.'*" Of course it was awkward, but it gave Sarah Joy and Brad an opportunity to discuss their relationship.

"We hadn't defined the relationship. Whatever you want to call it. We were just friends. Brad was getting ready to go to Law School. I was going to continue working as a nurse at the hospital. I had no plans to move. So, I was like, 'What am I supposed to tell my family?' Brad responded by saying, 'How about you tell them that we have a date this Saturday?'"

"*In the back of my mind I'd been thinking the whole summer 'This girl's awesome. This is exactly the kind of person that I want to be with.' But I was also thinking of Law School, especially with the first year being so demanding. It's going to be long distance. Can I make this work?*"

The next month, Brad left for Law School. "Long-distance is so tough on a relationship. We had a lot of people telling us long-distance relationships don't usually work. But for us, it drew us closer together. That space allowed us to pursue what we were pursuing. Every time he came home I felt like we fell more in love with each other. It was so hard every time we had to say goodbye."

"*I think it helped me actually perform as well as I did my first year of school. I ended up doing really, really well and part of that was being time pressured. I always made sure to do my homework before class, because I wanted to make sure that weekend I would be free to go home and visit Sarah Joy.*"

Sarah Joy and Brad talked about marriage. Sarah Joy was ready, but Brad took a little longer to think about the balance of it all. "*My preconceived notion is that the man should always be working and should always be providing. So, getting married while I was in school was a very uncomfortable idea for me. I remember actually calling my dad. He's a very conservative guy, and I thought he would just agree with me and say 'Yeah, wait through school then ask.' I called him and he said, 'Yeah, yeah, maybe just go ahead and get married.'"*

"I knew I was not going to propose until I knew how I was doing in school. I looked at my grades at the end of the semester and said, 'alright I'm ready. I'm going to ask her to marry me.' So, I ended up proposing the night before I returned to school for the spring semester."

Sarah Joy and Brad were given great marriage advice as they prepared for marriage. "Go into your marriage expecting nothing and then you will be so happy when the unexpected happens. Every little thing that your husband does for you, you will be completely excited about it, and you'll appreciate it more because you weren't expecting it. You'll be a lot more thankful in your marriage."

They also read *The Meaning of Marriage* by Tim Keller. "He said that marriage is a commitment and a promise where you promise to choose to love the other person. I thought the idea of choosing to love was so weird at first, because I think of love as a feeling. But he explained, feelings come and go and you're eventually going to wake up one morning and you're not going to feel it. When you get married, you're promising to love that person, to make the choice to do those things

and make those sacrifices, and put that person first even when you're not feeling it. We knew that if that was something that we could really commit to, then our marriage can survive almost anything."

Sarah Joy and Brad were married in July of 2013.

"Going from long-distance to living together was a really big change. When I was single, I woke up in the morning and thought, 'hey what do I want to do today?' and then I did it. When we were married, I had to think of somebody else first. Probably the toughest thing about marriage, honestly, is learning to put somebody else first. There's a lot of self-sacrifice in marriage. We're still learning that."

"Communication is key. Most, if not all, of our arguments result from lack of communication. Men and women interpret things differently. We have learned it is very important to communicate our feelings and expectations to each other. When we form expectations and then don't tell each other about the expectations we have, it becomes an unrealistic expectation because we haven't communicated. When the other person doesn't meet our expectation that we set, we get mad. The other person doesn't know why we're mad because we haven't told them what we expected in the first place, and then we end up fighting over something we never even talked about. It happens."

"One of my favorite things about being married is having a partner."

"In marriage, you have this person who is promising to stay by your side. You have a real partner in crime, somebody that you can always go to; somebody who is going to be there with you and for you. That is something that no other relationship can really do."

"I would encourage

any couple who is trying to balance demanding school and working careers, to try and look forward and focus. Let it be something that encourages you. The sacrifices that Sarah Joy has made for me and our family have encouraged me to work hard, stay focused, and keep my eyes on the prize. It has motivated me."

"I look forward to being settled with Brad and raising a family. Right now, we're on a big adventure of getting through Law School." ♥

"Probably the toughest thing about marriage, honestly, is learning to put somebody else first. There's a lot of self-sacrifice in marriage. We're still learning that."

JAY *and* JANE

MARRIED 27 YEARS
KANSAS CITY, MISSOURI

"When we realized we are in this forever and in this together, we learned to intentionally continue to get to know one another. At every stage of life, we have changed and we have different needs. We have to listen to each other. It is important to communicate and pay attention to get to know one another's needs and understand what we can and cannot do anymore. Knowing these things about each other helps us love one another where we are in that stage of life."

"An amazing marriage is laughing, crying, and just doing life together. This is my partner and I wouldn't want to do life with anybody else." ♥

JENNIFER *and* DAVID

MARRIED 2 YEARS
ST. LOUIS, MISSOURI

"We have fun, make each other laugh, and just love life together. Living with someone who understands you better than anyone else in the world provides an amazing blanket of comfort." ♥

ASHLEY *and* JEREMY

MARRIED 14 YEARS
KANSAS CITY, MISSOURI

"Our love story...It's on going."

During Ashley's freshman year of college, her friends recommended she email this guy named, Jeremy. Jeremy was a friend of Ashley's friends and was living in Hawaii for a short period of time. Little did Ashley know, they were recommending to Jeremy that he reach out to Ashley as well. They would say things like, "you are going to love her." Ashley was hesitant at first to "email a boy," but eventually she did.

"I wrote him and he wrote back, and we started writing letters… very very long letters and very honest. I mean, I guess we were kids, so we were just pen pals, but we were pen pals that were supposed to be soulmates. We were meant to be together and that started making itself very clear. Every single sentence he would write, I'd be like 'Oh me too!!! You just get me!!!'"

Eventually they started talking on the phone. They talked for hours using pay phones and phone cards while sitting on the pavement for hours, rain or shine. *"One time we talked until really, really late at night, and Ashley was like 'I need to go to bed, the sun is coming up.'"*

At one point, they knew they were going to marry one another, but they hadn't even seen a picture of each other yet. During one of their phone conversations, Jeremy said, "I'm going to marry you." Then Ashley said, "I know, I am probably going to marry you too… should we send each other photos?" So they did.

"When you have the chance to get to know someone's spirit, and their soul, before you have a chance to get to know their body, at that point, everything else is just like, 'Oh cool.' It was wonderful to think, 'I believe in this guy; I believe in who he is; I know I am going to be his wife; and it will be fun to see what he looks like too.'"

"It was really almost an out-of-body experience of this complete and total comfort, without any fear or reservation, from thousands of miles away."

"It was a safe place to land. Isn't that what marriage is? You are just hoping for a safe place to land at the end of the day. You are just hoping to really be seen for who you actually are, and for the answer to always be yes back."

"We had that yes before we even saw each other. I love that no matter what happens, and what has happened to our physical bodies, and what will continue to happen, that there is still that deep yes for the other person's soul and their spirit."

"I remember standing in the bathroom about 30 minutes before Jeremy's plane was expected to land, looking in the mirror and thinking, 'oh my gosh, I'm about to meet this person that I am in love with, and that I'm going to spend the rest of my life with. Oh my gosh. I need more lipstick.' So probably by the time he stepped off the plane, I looked like a grandma, with lipstick on my teeth and cheeks. I didn't know what else to do besides put on more lipstick. He walked off the plane and I just remember the feeling of his arms around my sides and around the small of my back. I remember taking my hand and touching the back of his head. It was a feeling of home. He grabbed my hand, and we walked out of the airport proudly."

Ashley and Jeremy's relationship moved quickly. Ashley first wrote to Jeremy in June. They met for the first time in September. Jeremy proposed in November, and they were married the following July.

"Soulmates are just two people willing to say 'okay, today I'll fight for us. You can give up, but I'm going to keep fighting for us. And then tomorrow, I'm not going to be strong enough to fight anymore, so you pick up the gloves and keep fighting for us then. Let's just not both give up at once, and then we will be okay.' Then the day that we do both give up at once, we will feel that divine presence of God coming in saying, 'Okay, here I will carry you because I made something really great and I am still creating it. I'm still getting really creative with it. I am going to paint in some really messed up contrasts that you didn't expect, but that's okay because it's going to make it better.'"

"One of my favorite moments in our marriage, was also one of the worst moments of our lives. We had gone to Colorado with our six-pound baby son, Zion, whom we had recently adopted. He was born premature and had brain trauma. We got to Colorado and the pressure in his brain became too much. Within about an hour, he went from being a normal baby to not breathing. His heart stopped. I did CPR in the back of our car, while Jeremy ran every light to get to the emergency room in time. We passed the baby off, and they took him to start doing spinal taps. They put him on oxygen, trying to get him to breathe again."

"I remember feeling like this isn't going to be okay. If we lose him, I don't know how this is going to be okay. I don't know how we stick together. Zion went through brain surgery. We had to cancel a workshop and call people who were on airplanes from overseas to come to a photography workshop in the mountains with us. We had already purchased almost all of the supplies. We were out so much money at this point, and we were in Colorado, which meant we weren't on Missouri Medicaid. All of these things that were happening were going to cost us more money than we could ever imagine having in a lifetime."

"There was a moment that night in the hospital where I looked at Jeremy and he looked at me. I just knew that was our crucial moment. That was a moment that neither one of us expected; neither one of us knew what to do, or how to survive. We had a decision to make. We had to choose that this marriage and this life is worth it. We had to stick together to survive. Or, we could have chosen to give up and we wouldn't come out of it together. We were both in this cloud of hopelessness. We realized our own powerlessness. We were either going to be in it together, or we were going to literally feel dead, and do it alone. The only way that we could have survived that was having the other one to prop us up."

"I remember having to choose to hold Jeremy's hand that night. What a difference from the day we first met. Jeremy grabbed my hand in the airport and off we walked to this beautiful life together of whimsy, joy, and perfection. Here we sat in a hospital room where our third son could die right in front of our eyes at any minute, and I had to make the choice to put my hand out and ask for Jeremy to hold it. I just remember the feeling of that night so clearly. We watched Zion on a breathing machine, five feet away, in his plastic incubator. As we held each other and cried, I remember thinking, 'I don't know how this one ends. But, I guess it ends with us together.'"

As strange as this sounds, this experience is one of my favorite, most horrible gut-wrenching things that happened to us. If it didn't happen, we wouldn't be sitting here. I think some other stupid little thing would have torn us apart. Our story needed this. We were stubborn, selfish, and determined that we could do this life on our own. God knew better that we couldn't."

"That was definitely our 'for better or for worse' moment. We made that vow when we got married, and simultaneously taught by our culture, 'it's always for better.'"

"The universe is wide open and God makes what He makes. Some of it is horrific, and you have to look away from it, while some of it is so beautiful

that your heart explodes out of your chest and you feel you might as well be in heaven. We have to be willing to take the bitter with the sweet. Marriage vows are real, and they become way more real when you're in the midst of horrific."

"That experience with Zion was such a gift, because it taught us how to humanize the other person. I no longer expect Jeremy to be perfect. I just expect him to be this man who's my husband. He's a very broken man, and he's very much my husband. I no longer expect that Jeremy is going to think that I'm this perfect put-together supermodel of a woman, who can carry herself with grace and poise all the time. He has seen all of my broken places and I'm going to just be a woman. I'm just going to be his wife. There's a lot of freedom in that. I don't need him to be perfect anymore. I can just love him for who he is. I can love the whole package; the beautiful and broken man that he is, and I don't need to fix that. I just have to see it and accept it as a gift to me… a gift to my life."

"The ground that our relationship has been built on is the unwavering, unconditional love of God. We believe there is a force in the universe that's powerful enough to fill us with so much love and belonging, to the point where we just overflow. That overflow spills onto one another and to our children, and onto our friends and family. I think that when we found that, and opened our hearts to that love, not judging it or labeling it, or trying to fit it into some pretty little weird 'American' box, but just letting it be real to us, we were able to see and be seen. We were able to be who we really are, just beautiful screw-ups. We now accept one another for that, joyfully."

"There is this ongoing joy of belonging to someone. Yesterday, we had some time to just be the two of us. The kids weren't in the house, and we were just like kids again. Just enjoying time. Those little moments are building blocks in our marriage that make it so strong and so powerful. They are my favorite every time." ♥

"Soulmates are just two people willing to say 'okay, today I'll fight for us. You can give up, but I'm going to keep fighting for us. And then tomorrow, I'm not going to be strong enough to fight anymore, so you pick up the gloves and keep fighting for us then. Let's just not both give up at once, and then we will be okay.'"

JENNY *and* JOSH

MARRIED 13 YEARS
RAYMORE, MISSOURI

"As a guy, it is in my human nature to always feel like I can fix things. I have finally come to the realization that sometimes there is a lot of crap in our life that we can't change. Properly communicating about our needs has been huge for us. Jenny may just need me to listen. And if that is all she needs from me, I can do that." ♥

MARY BETH *and* KEN

MARRIED 32 YEARS
BILLINGS, MONTANA

While Ken was a senior in college and Mary Beth was a senior in high school, they both worked at a little family diner in town called, *The Happy Diner*. They were just friends at first, but over time, their relationship developed. One night after work when Mary Beth was waiting for her dad to pick her up, she ran up to Ken and kissed him.

"It was just this innocent little kiss in the parking lot and that was just kind of the start. I was pretty forward. My mom always taught me to go after what I want."

"*Mary Beth was always way ahead of me in terms of where our relationship was going to go, because my head was always in school. I was focused on trying to finish school and get a job.*"

"I knew after about six months that I was maturely in love with him. He was drop dead gorgeous. He was a lot like my dad: respectful, hardworking, and loyal."

After Ken finished his Graduate School Program,

they were married on September 9, 1983. They knew they wanted to have children, but they struggled to stay pregnant. They moved to Idaho and miscarried at three months, then moved to Bozeman and miscarried again after three months, then came back to Billings and again miscarried at three months.

"We started to feel a little desperate about whether or not we would have kids or not. It strained our relationship. Mary Beth was going through something so horrific and painful and my heart was just going out to her. The woman I loved, who was carrying our child was hooked up to this machine having a D&C procedure against her will. Knowing we were losing a child we had been putting our hopes on was really tough. Those are the kind of moments where you realize how important that person is to you. You go along for months at a time just taking each other for granted and then you have those jolts in your world, when something scary happens, and you go 'Whoa, wait a second. What would I do if she wasn't here tomorrow?"

"This is something that we have learned over the 32 years of marriage: we are not always going to be healthy, nor will we always be around. So we should probably try to enjoy things while we can."

"My favorite thing about marriage is having a partner that I can rely on and a best friend that will always be there. Someone who will always love me no matter what I look like on Sunday mornings. It's stability in my life. It is not hot passionate romantic love anymore. It's a constant and something we can always rely on."

"We were taught to fake it till you make it. Marriage is just like anything that you are good at. Just because you are good at it doesn't mean you don't have to work at it. Always ask for help."

"An amazing marriage is a long life together. It gets better with time." ♥

"This is something that we have learned over the 32 years of marriage: we are not always going to be healthy nor will we always be around. So, we should probably try to enjoy things while we can."

EMMY *and* JOHN

MARRIED 8 YEARS
LINCOLN, NEBRASKA

While living in Madison, Wisconsin, Emmy and John were introduced to one another by their mutual friend, Jessica. After an evening of hanging out with a group, Emmy and John exchanged numbers. They went out on their first date the next Friday, the day after Emmy broke her arm snowboarding. "I was in a 90 degree cast and had to have a friend help me get dressed, put my hair in a ponytail, and put toothpaste on my toothbrush. I wasn't going to miss this date!" They hit it off and continued to date for about eight months before John proposed.

Emmy always admired her grandparents' marriage. "After my grandmother met John, she said, 'you know, he reminds me so much of your grandfather.' I remember thinking 'Yes! That's what I want. I want what they had.' I don't know if she was meaning to bless our relationship, but in my mind, it was very much like that."

Emmy and John were married in Emmy's hometown in Minnesota in 2007. They settled into their careers in Madison and welcomed their son, Braden Charles, to their family in 2009. "In July 2010, we found out we were expecting another little boy. At this point we started re-evaluating our life in Madison. With two demanding careers and soon-to-be two children, we felt that we wanted to explore moving to a location where we would have more support from our families." In September of that year, John accepted a position in Lincoln, Nebraska, and they made the move closer to John's family.

"During the next year and a half, I stayed home with the boys. Although I enjoyed my time at home with them, I was feeling defeated that I had been unable to find a teaching position here in Nebraska, and I felt a bit lost and lonely. During that time, I began dreaming about my future and what I should do next... go back to teaching, back to Graduate School again, or start the business that I had always been crazy about, opening a bridal store. After writing a business plan and working on my daydream full-time, I opened Blush Bridal Boutique in October of 2012."

During this time, Emmy and John have learned the importance of taking turns. "When we moved to Lincoln, I stepped back from my career so John could cultivate his. When I started my business, it became my turn to focus on my career and John took a step back. At this point, I have the flexibility in my business that I am able to take a step away while John is focused on his job. I firmly believe, you can have everything, but you can't do everything at the same time!"

"*Being in a supportive relationship has given us the confidence, opportunity, and encouragement that we need to follow our dreams. It has made us better personally and professionally.*"

"Before we were married, we talked about what

was important to us. Holding true to our values and what we wanted out of our marriage, we knew we wanted to be near family and support each other's interests. We have both made sacrifices to get to the place where we started out knowing we wanted to be."

"Some of the best advice we can give is to support each other's passions. The thing that makes people happy is doing what they are passionate about, like working in a certain area or spending a Saturday fishing. Support each other's passions and know what they are. That relies on communication and a willingness to understand what the other person is thinking, where they are in terms of what they are looking for, and/or what they need at this point."

"My favorite thing about marriage is the journey. Our marriage is different than it was when it started and I am sure it will be different five years from now. It is more about enjoying every moment. Today those moments include the little moments of us hanging out with our boys in the backyard, playing baseball. Five years from now it will be something different. In work and career, I always look ahead and plan ahead. But personally, I try to savor the moment. Savor what we have now, because life is fleeting."

"An amazing marriage is fun. It is suppose to be fun. Life is too short to worry about the small things that often get in your face, like problems that will be gone in a day, or problems where a year from now you won't remember what the fight was about. It's more about enjoying each other's time together." ♥

"My favorite thing about marriage is the journey. Our marriage is different than it was when it started, and I am sure it will be different five years from now. It is more about enjoying every moment."

JESSIE *and* JASON

MARRIED 18 YEARS
LAS VEGAS, NEVADA

Jessie and Jason met when they were 16 years old at a church convention in Long Island, New York. After seeing each other two weekends in a row at the convention, they exchanged addresses and telephone numbers. "This was back in 1993, when we didn't have cell phones or Skype, so we wrote lots of letters back and forth." Jessie lived in Maryland, about a five hour drive from Long Island.

"I remember the first time Jason called my house, he had to go to a pay phone because he was scared his parents would freak out if they saw a long distance call on their bill. He kept getting prompted by the operator to add more change to continue the call. Clearly it was not the most romantic phone call. It was so much fun though, and at that point, at my young age of 16, I knew he was special."

Jessie and Jason wrote letters back and forth and continued to call each other over the years. Jason took every opportunity and long weekend in high school to visit Jessie, taking trains and catching rides.

Two years later, Jessie's family decided to move to Florida to be closer to her sister. "I was excited to get out of rural Maryland, but sad to be leaving Jason. Even though we were only 18 years old, we'd been doing our long distance relationship for two years and it was going good. We moved in December of 1995 to Kissimmee. Jason drove

with us, and it was a very sad goodbye. A few months later, he drove from New York to Florida to visit, and after about two semesters in college in New York, it was no surprise to anyone that he transferred to Florida to be with me. I was beyond happy to have Jason live just 20 minutes away."

Instead of waiting until they graduated from college, Jessie and Jason decided they wanted to be together. At the very "tender" age of 19, they were married.

"Jason and I grew up together. We went to school, worked full-time, and we somehow made it work on a very small budget. It's funny to look back now and see how fearless and full of hope we were."

"Being married at such a young age was definitely a huge obstacle. The odds were not in our favor. We argued a lot about everything. It would have been really easy to just give up and go our separate ways. But we didn't. We kept at it. We learned to live with each other. We learned that compromising doesn't mean losing. We learned that it's okay to make small changes for the one we love. We overcame growing apart and grew together as adults."

"Jason started talking about wanting to have children around the age of 27. He really had to convince me, because I was not ready to give up my freedom for children. Before deciding to be a mom, I knew I didn't want my life to revolve strictly around my child, and I knew I didn't want our relationship to suffer. We made a very intentional effort to go on dates and spend quality time together."

Jessie and Jason always knew they wanted to raise their children with family close. So, when Jessie's parents decided to move from Florida to Las Vegas, they said yes to adventure, and moved there too.

"We've been here for six years and really enjoy the life we're making. We continue to date, our love for each other is stronger than ever, and we are very intentional with our life. We strive to have a fun family life and travel as much as possible with our kiddos, but we also make it a point to travel without them at least once or twice a year too!"

"We can get so busy with life, bills, and the routine, that we forget to breathe sometimes. It's so important to spend quality time together without distractions. We talk about our dreams and make plans for them together."

"An amazing marriage is one that requires a little bit of work, but is also a lot of fun." ♥

"It would have been really easy to just give up and go our separate ways. But we didn't. We kept at it. We learned to live with each other. We learned that compromising doesn't mean losing. We learned that it's okay to make small changes for the one we love. We overcame growing apart and grew together as adults."

AMANDA *and* TYLER

MARRIED 5 YEARS
DOVER, NEW HAMPSHIRE

In sixth grade, Tyler moved to Amanda's hometown. "He was adorable and every girl had a crush on him. During the last slow song of the last school dance of the year, I don't know what came over me, but I walked right over to him and asked him to dance. This was so out of character for me, thank God he said yes. We spun awkwardly in circles for the duration of the song and then parted ways to go back to our friends. A few days later, we started going out. This lasted a few short months, and during the Summer, he had his friend Cat (the best man in our wedding) call me at my friend's house to break up with me. I was sad, okay heartbroken, but I was 11 years old, so I managed to move on!"

After years of not really talking or hanging out, Tyler ended up at Amanda's house with a group of friends. "It was the beginning of a great friendship, which a few months later turned into a romantic relationship. No one, and I mean NO ONE ever saw Ty and I being in a relationship. I played soccer, was a class officer, and participated in anything I could. Ty could have cared less about high school or his 10 year plan. I guess you could say opposites attract. We were exactly what the other needed. I made him a little more serious and he made me a little more spontaneous. He ended up participating in spirit week and doing community service with me, and I ended up ditching one or two classes to do something exciting with him. We were smitten!"

Amanda and Tyler continued dating throughout high school and applied to all of the same colleges to assure they would remain close to each other and continue their relationship.

"We grew up together during those four years of college. Right before we graduated, we broke up for a few months and saw other people. I wanted to make sure we belonged together and weren't just staying together because it was safe. We had been together since we were 16, and I knew the next step would be staying together for a lifetime."

"Needless to say, we ended up back together two months later. Getting back together was hard. It felt weird and there was some jealousy and hurt. We certainly realized everyone else we had dated during this period was like a vacation, but Ty and I were like home."

About three years later, Amanda and Tyler built a house together, got engaged, and then married. "We started our careers, got new jobs, and new cars. We did all the things you were supposed to do in our 20s and were each other's best friends while we did it all. This is not to say this time was without heartache. We had two miscarriages during this time, some very serious health scares with our immediate family, and some out of character trust issues. We had a solid year of things just knocking us down and pushing us back, both out of our control and in our control.

125

We vowed to stick together. We have always made our relationship a priority, but we had to kick it into overdrive that year."

"Although we had our highs and extreme lows while attempting to have a baby, we never gave up hope and knew that one day that wish would come true. In September 2013, we found out that we were once again pregnant and that same joy we had during the previous times we felt again. Although we were both overcome with joy and happiness, the heartaches we had experienced in the past were always in the back of our minds. As the months went by, these concerns began to fade and it became more and more a reality that this time it was meant to be. On May 14, 2014, we were blessed with our little boy, Asher Michael Parkhurst. We were fairly clueless on how to raise a child, but we worked hard as a team and took it day-by-day. The next year and a half was the most exhausting, fast paced, and love-filled time we have encountered, and I could not be more happy that we were able to experience it all together."

"Marriage is hard. It is so easy to get into a routine where you don't really appreciate each other, the romance really isn't there, and there is no spark. We work, come home, cook dinner, play with our son, sit down, and watch T.V. There really isn't any romance in that. The hard part is making sure that we stay connected. I feel like we can get lost in other things that are happening so easily, that keeping the romance alive is probably our biggest struggle."

"We have a lot of balls in the air as we juggle life. We are trying to keep up with a very energetic and sweet little boy, while taking a leap of faith and changing our life plan. I have recently quit my job as a teacher, a career I have thought about since I was five, to become a barista. We are three weeks away from opening our first business together. We have never been more unsure about where life is taking us, and it is both exciting and terrifying. We are quite certain about one thing, and that is each other. We are still trying to figure out how to be grown ups, but we will keep growing just like we have been doing for the past 15 years...together."

"An amazing marriage is experiencing life's journey: the good, bad, and the amazing with your best friend." ♥

"Marriage is hard.
It is so easy to get into a routine
where you don't really appreciate
each other, the romance really
isn't there, and there is no spark.
We work, come home, cook
dinner, play with our son, sit
down, and watch T.V. There
really isn't any romance in that.
The hard part is making sure
that we stay connected."

KIM *and* JOSH

MARRIED 3 YEARS
LEBANON, NEW HAMPSHIRE

"Being flexible and adapting to the ever-changing conditions in both of our lives is key. We have to check-in with each other frequently, be willing to adjust from our 'norms' and recognize that our marriage is going to grow and change as we move forward. Relationships are always a work in progress." ♥

DANICA *and* LUKE

MARRIED 4 YEARS
NEWARK, NJ

Danica and Luke met on December 13, 1997 when they were 17 years old. They were both working at the local movie theatre.

"*Before my first day of work at the theatre, a friend of mine told me that there was this very, very pretty girl who worked there. He said, 'she is a good girl.' When I saw Danica, I instantly knew that was the girl he was talking about.*

The beauty that my friend was talking about, wasn't really the physical beauty. Danica was an authentic person. She was always nice and everything about her was so great. I knew that I wanted her as a wife from that first night we worked together."

"Our friendship was instant. He was fun to hang out with, but I wasn't interested."

They remained close friends and saw each other often. It wasn't until about four years after they met that they took their relationship to a different level. Danica was returning from Monmouth University and Luke was returning from his full-time duty in the military.

"Our friendship was better than a lot of my relationships. I always questioned why I couldn't find her type of qualities in a girlfriend. She was already coming to Thanksgiving with my mom as a friend. She won that respect as a friend. I found that no one else could live up to Danica. It was the first time that anyone besides my family treated me as equal. At that point, I realized she is definitely quality and I definitely wanted to keep her around longer."

"I think we started hugging intimately at the start. I heard so many times how relationships can ruin friendships and one thing I knew for sure is that I wanted her friendship in my life always. We didn't want to mess it up."

"I think our marriage is so resilient because we established a strong friendship before we were romantically involved. Our friendship is solid."

"We had our first son in 2004 and decided to finally get married in 2011. We didn't live together until we got married. There were a lot of spiritual and moral things that were going on. Amongst the marriage counseling, it got rocky because there were still some things we were butting heads against. However, we did it. We did it backwards, and it is not traditional, but I wouldn't have wanted it any other way. It was a special experience to have our six-year-old son in our wedding."

Luke grew up with a single mom working hard to support her children. *"It was hard for me growing up without seeing that partnership between a mother and a father, or husband and wife. I have never had a woman expect much of me. I was used to people saying, 'you are cool because you look cool or because you are driving a cool car.' But never has someone seen the qualities as far as honor, dignity, and respect. No one saw those types of characteristics in me until Danica brought it to the forefront."*

"I didn't want to be a statistic. I didn't want to be someone's baby momma. I saw those qualities in Luke, and I wanted to carry on his legacy. I could see the type of person he is. I wanted to have a family with him."

Danica and Luke conceived their second son on their honeymoon. "The most exciting thing we have been through together is watching our children grow. Since Luke grew up without his father around, he is particularly protective of his relationship with his boys. It's amazing to see them together, and to see the love and respect they have for each other."

"The biggest challenge we have faced together is the loss of our third son, on September 3, 2015. It was determined during our first trimester screening that the baby had a heart defect and possible chromosome abnormalities. I never got further testing because either way we were going to continue with the pregnancy. At my 28-week visit with the doctor, it was determined that the baby's heart did stop beating. I delivered my third son and life has changed since. It hasn't been an easy healing journey, but God's grace and love has continued to sustain us and make us stronger."

"I wasn't really sensitive to things like death and misfortune because I always felt like I grew up with misfortune. I didn't carry the baby. As men,

we don't have that instant bond. Danica is my baby and whoever she is carrying is my baby. But, I was so busy taking care of work and the household, I didn't take time to be sensitive to the situation. It wasn't until after the stillbirth that I realized I needed to be more sensitive. Even though I didn't physically go through it, that situation gave me a feeling of sensitivity and compassion. Men deal with physical and logical. Women deal from the heart, and sometimes things will harbor longer in a woman than it would in a man. I realized I needed to get out of my shelter and be there for her."

"We have our ups and downs like any other married couple. We miscommunicate, misunderstand each other, love each other, can't stand each other, forget that we are a couple because we are busy being parents, forget to date, dream together, argue, make love, disappoint and forgive. Many of our friends who have known us for years say we have the perfect marriage. They are wrong. It's perfectly imperfect. We roll with the punches, and we never give up. There are days when we can't stand each other, but we don't throw in the towel. It's not easy. It is a responsibility, especially as a parent. We have to set the example. What our kids see is what they are going to model after. Marriage is not a fad. It's not

just something to do because everyone else is doing it. For us, marriage is proof that we believe that our spouse is worth the effort."

"An amazing marriage to us is a marriage that involves two people giving 100%. It's never 50/50. It is giving 100% of oneself, in commitment, respect, and love." ♥

"Marriage is not a fad. It's not just something to do because everyone else is doing it. For us, marriage is proof that we believe that our spouse is worth the effort."

SHREYA *and* SOUGATA

MARRIED 10 YEARS
PRINCETON, NEW JERSEY

"I don't have words to describe what I feel, but when Shreya is not around, I feel an emptiness that I can't fill with whatever I choose to do. I can fill my day with stuff, but it still will not take over for that emptiness that I feel when she is not around. I can't quite describe what that is. I call it constant companionship. 'I am because you are.' I don't see myself living or existing without her." ♥

LEIGH *and* MICHAEL

MARRIED 19 YEARS
SANTE FE, NEW MEXICO

"We met in church while living in Colorado. We both had grown up in Texas, so we had a lot in common. We were best friends for about two years. I always thought whoever marries Michael is going to be really blessed. I never really put myself into the equation."

Michael, who had already fallen for Leigh, waited patiently for her. Leigh's eyes were opened when Michael asked her to go on a date, without the group they were used to hanging out with. "I knew when he kissed me and told me he loved me, that it was the real thing."

They were engaged shortly after and then married eight months later.

The past 19 years have been nothing short of adventurous for Leigh and Michael. Between river rafting class IV rapids in Colorado, skiing their way thru British Columbia, kayaking the coastline of the Island of Maui, driving cross-country in their truck and 33 foot Fifth Wheel, roller blading thru Denver, and riding horses bareback in the Caribbean Sea, these two have certainly experienced adventure.

Amongst the travel and exploring, Leigh and Michael put down their roots in Santa Fe, New Mexico. They purchased a new home together and ran a successful Push-Cart Business, selling delicious Kettle Corn on the historic Plaza in Santa Fe, New Mexico.

"Being an entrepreneur requires a lot of fortitude. Determination will take you far, but for us, it has been much more than that. Total reliance on the Lord has made the difference. Running a Push-Cart in a six by nine foot space, setting up and breaking down a store every day, and working 10-14 hour days for years in all kinds of weather and circumstances is absolutely exhausting."

"Running a business together has been very challenging on our marriage because when you're working together, there's nobody else to blame except each other, and that's a hard dynamic in a marriage. We were never really argumentative before. We were best friends before we were married and I think that's something we always have to remember."

"Our secret to a happy marriage starts with forgiveness. Forgiveness infuses hope into your marriage. People do make mistakes and they will disappoint you. What forgiveness does is starts the process to allow two people to begin to work together and not against each other. And you really have to practice forgiveness. It's a practice."

In the balance of running a business together and focusing on their marriage, Leigh and Michael have learned to keep it simple and minimize the distractions in their lives. "The main issues that bring pressure are usually from an external force. That is why we always have to keep coming back to talk to each other. We are always questioning: What is our main focus? Where are we going? How can we change things and mix things up, so that we are not being so pulled and inundated?"

The good news is, "whatever challenging situation you find yourself in, it's not going to be that way a year from now. It's going to change."

"The advice we would give to any couple would be to pick up a copy of the Bible. If you want a great adventure together, then open the book and look up John 14:6 in the New Testament. Keep on reading and let the adventure begin!"

"An amazing marriage to us is a successful triangle between a man, a woman, and God!" ▾

MILLIE *and* RICHARD

MARRIED 57 YEARS
BRONXVILLE, NEW YORK

"We met when I was 15 years old and he had seen me around the neighborhood. As soon as he laid his eyes on me, he wanted to meet me. A mutual friend introduced us. Richie asked me out, so we started going out pretty regularly. We went for rides together and to get a bite to eat. We loved going on long rides. From that point on, we knew we wanted to be together."

"Richie went into the service for a couple years, and we got married soon after he came back. I was only 20 years old, but we loved each other so much."

Millie and Richard had three children together. "In the beginning we said we would have 10 kids, but then after three, we said 'no way.' There is nothing in the world like building a family together. Without a doubt in our mind, having our children and our grandchildren is the most exciting thing we have done together. We didn't even realize how much we could love each other until we had kids together. Building a family from pure love is our greatest accomplishment. There was never a shortage of love in our house."

"There was a time we were both sick and out of work. We almost lost our house. We had no money coming in and we had three young kids. Kids need things like food and comfort. We fought a lot then and that wasn't something we normally did. We kept fighting, but we figured it out. We had to be strong for each other and for our kids, so we did. We made it through."

"In order to get through the challenges, we have learned that we can't take marriage lightly. We have to really truly be in love and feel like we can't even live without that other person by our side. It won't work unless we truly love each other and are committed to each other."

"Being with someone you love every day is the best part of marriage. I get to share my life with my best friend. Not many people get to say that. I am so lucky to be so in love with the person I get to spend every day with. I love loving him. We love going for long rides and walks together. But our favorite thing, of course, is to be with our family. There is no feeling like the one when our kids and grandkids are all together. It's a room full of so much love, and it all started with us."

"You want your husband to be happy. He wants you to be happy. I don't think it's so hard or complicated if you just look at it the easy way. You just want each other to be happy, so you try to work towards that goal of making each other happy."

"An amazing marriage to us is knowing that we have each other, always. It's being with someone that you are madly in love with, every day, forever. I've loved him every day for 57 years and will every day after. That's amazing, and it only gets more amazing everyday!" ♥

"There is no feeling like the one when our kids and grandkids are all together. It's a room full of so much love, and it all started with us."

JENNIFER *and* ROLANDO

MARRIED 7 YEARS
NEW YORK, NEW YORK

"There were a lot of skeptics amongst our friends and family, who judged our young age, but we are proud to say we have proved them wrong so far. In the 12 years we have been together, we have graduated high school and college, started careers, opened a business and bought a home (also can't forget being parents to our 10-year-old pup, RJ!). We attribute being able to do all of this because of each other. We have supported each other and held each other up through every success, challenge, and failure." ♥

BETSY *and* BILL

MARRIED 36 YEARS
CHARLOTTE, NORTH CAROLINA

"Bill moved to my hometown, Lenox, Massachusetts while we were in high school. Bill was in tenth grade and I was in eighth. He and my brother became great friends. When he came over to the house, I notice him a lot. Eventually, he noticed me. We started dating in 1970. For me it was the most wonderful time of my life!"

Bill went to college in North Carolina, while Betsy remained in Massachusetts to finish high school. Eventually, Betsy went to college in Upstate New York, and then transferred to Hood College in Maryland. Bill started his career with a job at General Electric and moved around for a training program. Betsy graduated from college and they married in July. After high school until they were married, they had never lived in the same place at the same time. When they came home from their honeymoon, they flew into Tampa, Florida and started their lives together. "We really got to know each other and become good friends. We had a lot of time to grow up and have fun together." Fourteen years, and two daughters later, Bill's job took them to Farmington Hills, Michigan, where they welcomed their third child, Luke.

"During Luke's birth, his heart stopped for six minutes, leaving him with severe brain damage. He was physically and mentally disabled and spent his first month in the hospital. We were told he would only live for a couple of years,

and we were encouraged to put him in a special facility for significantly disabled kids. We brought him home, and from that point forward, we were his caregivers. We fed him with a special tube every four hours around the clock. We weren't really husband and wife during that time of our lives. We were teachers, caregivers, doctors, therapists, and nurses. However, Luke brought us a lot of joy because he was a very happy child. The girls adored their brother."

When Luke was four years old, they moved to Charlotte, North Carolina. "We had to make a lot of decisions during this time. We made the choice very early on that we would always make decisions with the information that we had at the time, and we would make the decision we believed would be in Luke's best interest and ours. We decided to never look back and second-guess ourselves because you learn as you go."

In 1998, Luke passed away. "*The birth and death of our son was life changing. We got by with a lot of help from family and friends. We had to learn how our family would go forward. Betsy went from having a full-time responsibility to having an empty house and girls who were active and out with their friends.*"

"It was a challenge for me. I got lost in grief to a point that was horrible. Through time and just giving each other space without trying to solve everything for each other, we made it through that difficult time in our marriage."

In 2001, Bill lost his job and just five months later, Betsy was diagnosed with stage two Breast Cancer. She went through two years of treatment, and five years later was told she was cancer free. However, in December 2009, the disease returned, and this time she was diagnosed with stage four cancer that had metastasized.

"My cancer has been managed well for over four years. But there is always a fear of what can happen, knowing this disease is forever now. I hate the thought of missing out on grandkids, and the thought of my girls and Bill having to deal with the sadness of death again."

"*Cancer being something that is all pervasive now, I have had to adjust the way I approach things. A big part of that has been listening and being sensitive to what it is that Betsy wants. My approach had been, 'Betsy is sick, so I am going to take care of everything. I am going to cook; I am going to clean; I am going to do this and that, and manage everything like it is a project with tasks that need to be taken care of.' I realized through some very direct feedback, that is not necessarily what Betsy needed. She also didn't need me to try to solve things, or try to tell her how to feel. It was a process, but I learned that sometimes if we are sitting on the couch, she doesn't need me to jump up and grab the vacuum cleaner, even if we need to vacuum. Sometimes she needs me to just sit there with her, whether we talk or not. My heart was in the right place, but I didn't need to be a whirlwind of activity. I could give myself a break too, and by doing that, it kind of gave her one.*"

"We didn't communicate that until it became an issue. All I had to do was tell him. I realized I can't assume that Bill knows everything. Even after all of these years, we still have to remind ourselves of that."

"*You have to be comfortable saying what you want. But also comfortable accepting what the other person needs.*"

"We learned that sometimes there is not going to be an agreement, but that doesn't mean that both of us are wrong or right, we just see things differently and handle things differently. We are always going to feel differently about different situations, and we have to respect what the other person in going through. Through communicating, we learn how to handle things a little bit better. We are always working hard on that one. We have been through so many different changes, and every situation that happens in our relationship makes us start all over again at the beginning. Every day is something different."

"Through all of these challenges, we have had ups and downs. Like all couples, we have had periods of time when we did not communicate well. We have had times of being angry and disappointed. But we have worked through them, because what we have is so worth keeping."

"We have fun. In spite of having things that come up that are difficult, Bill and I share a lot of moments where we laugh. I want to always be able to laugh and share the things that got us here. We have fun doing stuff for each other and with each other. When we do things that we love to do individually, our joy comes when we get to tell each other about that experience."

"An amazing marriage is living life with someone who has learned to be sensitive to what I like, what I need, and sometimes what I don't need." ♥

"You have to be comfortable saying what you want. But also comfortable accepting what the other person needs."

ALECIA *and* TAYLOR

MARRIED 2 YEARS
GACKLE, NORTH DAKOTA

"We have known each other since kindergarten. My first memory of Taylor is talking about *Scooby Doo* in first grade."

Alecia and Taylor grew up in a small community where everyone knew everyone. Their graduating class was the largest in the school and had 12 students.

"When senior prom rolled around, I was date-less and I wanted to ask Taylor to prom. So, I asked my best friend for his cell phone number, so I could text him. She gave me his number and I texted him right away, because it was getting late. I didn't get a reply. Later, I found out, the number I texted was actually Taylor's old phone, which was now his mom's."

They went to the prom with separate dates, but did end up sharing a few dances together, including, Jason Aldean's '*Big Green Tractor.*'

"I know it is strange, but I just had the weirdest feeling when we danced to that song. Like, I fell in love, then and there."

Alecia and Taylor graduated from high school and didn't hang out again until Taylor started helping on Alecia's family farm that Summer. After riding the tractor together one day, they mutually agreed to go see a movie.

"During the movie, I was hoping I would be able to figure out exactly where we stood as a couple, or just friends. I was hoping he would make the moves, whatever those may be. So, about halfway through the movie, I finally decided that there was nothing between us and we were just friends. That all changed at the end of the movie, when Taylor offered me his hand to hold. I remember asking him 'Are you sure?' more than once. He then dropped me off at my parent's house, where he stayed to visit more. We were on our way to the pool outside, when he 'tripped' and we kissed under the stars."

Just a few weeks later, Alecia went off to college about two and a half hours away, while Taylor started his career on his parent's farm. Alecia came home often to visit and during her Winter Break of her last year in school, Taylor asked her to marry him. About a year and a half later, they were married, and now live on the farm Taylor's grandfather homesteaded. They have 370 cattle and 2,800 acres of grain.

"Growing up, I always said I am never marrying a farmer, because I knew the stress behind it since I grew up on a farm too. It is pretty much a gamble every year, because we never know what the weather is going to do. In farming, you either go into debt or stay the same. You are never really making money, because you are always just putting it back into the operation."

"Farming is a full-time 24/7 job. I learned fast

that cattle come first, before date nights, before church, before vacations, and before special events. We always have to be prepared for anything and everything, from calving in the below zero Winter months, to praying for rain in the middle of the Summer. Farming is never dull and has completely changed me. Growing up on a farm only slightly prepared me for the upgrade to a farmer's wife. It is stressful, but it is the only life I would want to live, especially with my farming husband by my side."

"It is a huge responsibility to be a farmer's wife. My wifely duties include: cooking, cleaning, raising a family, making sure everything is running smoothly, getting groceries, and making sure there is food in the fridge. Since I work

full-time as well, on the weekend I usually try to make some meals, so there are leftovers in the fridge for the week."

"After being diagnosed with Rheumatoid Arthritis at the age of 23, I often get worked up wondering if I will be able to uphold my wifely duties. Thankfully, I have an amazing and supportive husband by my side everyday."

Alecia and Taylor work very different schedules. Alecia commutes 55 miles one way to her job and Taylor works all the time on the farm. As a couple, they have decided to take Sunday as their day together.

"We go to church together, cook dinner together, and take naps together. It is our only day that we set aside during the week, minus technology and all of the other daily distractions, and just be with each other. In order for our marriage to be successful, we have to set time aside for one another. It is hard and requires sacrifice, but it is worth it for us."

"My favorite thing about being married is knowing that even if we don't get to see each other during the day, like during planting season and harvest, it's nice to know I share a bed with my better half. We are truly best friends and soulmates. Just knowing that I get to fall asleep and wake up with the love of my life is such a great feeling. It is nice to know we are never alone in this world and that we have each other. It is an amazing feeling." ♥

"It is a huge responsibility to be a farmer's wife. My wifely duties include: cooking, cleaning, raising a family, making sure everything is running smoothly, getting groceries, and making sure there is food in the fridge."

JUDY *and* PHIL

MARRIED 39 **YEARS**
COLUMBUS, OHIO

When Phil's family moved to a small fishing town in California, the principal at his new school called

Mr. O'Connor's fifth grade classroom to ask for a student to welcome the "new kid." "*All that I kept thinking in my head was 'let it be a boy. Let it be a boy. Let it be a boy,' so that I could meet a friend. And then it was Judy. We were always really good friends, and by our junior year of high school, we started dating.*" Judy and Phil attended the same college, but after three years of dating, they broke up. "*We really loved each other a lot. We just needed to do some individual growing. We just really needed to grow as people, rather than grow as a couple. At least we had the maturity to understand that.*"

During their breakup, they dated other people seriously, but continued to see one another as friends. After eight or nine months of not dating, they got together for a lunch. "*I had just broken up with a girl and Judy was still dating a fellow pretty seriously. During that lunch, we had realized that we had done some of the growing we knew we needed to do. Two things happened for me during that lunch. First, I realized that I was still deeply in love with Judy.*

And secondly, Judy told me that she thought her boyfriend was going to propose to her that weekend. We left that lunch and I realized I needed to marry Judy and there was a chance she might marry someone else."

Phil knew he needed to act fast. So, he wrote her a letter declaring his love to her. Two weeks later, they ran into each other. Phil worked up the courage to ask Judy if her boyfriend proposed to her. She said, "Yeah he did. But, I told him no, because I think I still love someone else." That was the moment they realized they were still deeply in love, and this time, they were going to date towards marriage.

Their relationship changed a lot. They both became Christians and decided to abstain from sexual relations until after they were married. *"The obedience of saying no to our desires was really powerful. Judy knew I had really strong desires for her physically. Prior to marriage, I wanted Judy to know that I could say no to myself. After we got married, I wanted her to know that I could say no outside of our marriage. I wanted to build that obedience of saying no for her sake. And she wanted to know that I could say that to myself. It was a good exercise of obedience. We wanted each other to know that the other person was worth waiting for."*

Within a year, Judy and Phil were engaged and married. *"On the day we got married, in so many ways, our marriage was better than my parent's marriage ever was. Judy would say we had a long way to go. Judy is the vision caster of what our marriage should be and could be, and I am very teachable and willing to make the plan come to fruition. My commitment to Judy was for her to be all that God wanted her to be, and to use me to help her do that. I take delight in seeing who she is and who she has become."*

"We are a product of our environment. More than we had any idea. As for most people, our family is the only family we know. However, it is not hardened cement. Going into marriage, our conflict styles were very different. She never saw her parents argue with one another. She also never heard them say, 'I love you.' My parents were young when they got married. There was lots of shouting, yelling, screaming, and even throwing things at each other. But, my parents were also very outward with their affection with one another. When Judy and I came together, we would agree that we were different. We could have said, 'this is my way. This is your way.' But you can't lean into just that. You have to be willing to say, 'we can break this chain and we can really do it differently.' Just because we came from knowing it one way, doesn't mean it's acceptable."

As parents themselves to three children, Judy and Phil knew they wanted to be a loving example of marriage to their children. *"We believe very strongly you don't give up your marriage for the sake of your children. We always wanted our children to know that we have an exclusive relationship. The best thing I can give to my children is a strong love for my wife."*

"I am really grateful that Phil kept pursuing me as we became parents. It is so easy to feel really rejected and not have the attention, or not feel the connection, because your wife is tending the kids. It is easy to feel like there is no time left for each other. As parents, it was common to get to the end of the day and just feel exhausted. It was so important for us to talk about it with each other when we were feeling disconnected. When it comes down to it, Phil is my partner for a lifetime."

"In a blink of an eye, our kids were graduating

high school, going to college, finding the 'love of their life' and getting married. Our decades in Columbus, Ohio helped us to create the kind of foundation for our marriage that would prepare us for the new stage of life, 'empty nesters.'"

"After a few months of adjustments when our kids left the house, we realized that we were still 'best friends' and that this stage of life really was special. Soon afterwards, we were offered an opportunity to join our oldest daughter, her husband, and kids, in an adventure of living in Tanzania, Africa. Phil retired from his job as an elementary school principal in a suburban school district, and we moved to Tanzania for two years. The kinds of challenging and amazing adventures we encountered in Africa brought all new ways for us to grow as a couple."

"Returning to Ohio after those two years, led us into our current phase of life, 'retirement.' This new phase has probably been the most enjoyable, overall. One blessing is having all three children, their spouses, and our seven grandchildren living in Columbus with us. We love this phase and believe we will have many more new adventures ahead of us as best friends and lovers."

"Our best advice for couples is to marry well, but don't expect it to be perfect. Making the choice of who you marry is possibly the most important decision you can make. Don't ever think that if your marriage takes some work, it's not a good marriage. All marriages take work, but it's the best investment of time and energy you can ever make. Be willing to make changes in yourself much, much, more than you expect your spouse to make changes. Surround yourself with people who know you, love you, and who will tell you when you're wrong. Always remember you have the possibility of spending your life with your best friend. So, treat the time together as if you are best friends."

"An amazing marriage is one that demonstrates mutual love and respect for each other. One that has both people working very hard to serve the needs of the other person." ▾

"Don't ever think that if your marriage takes some work, it's not a good marriage. All marriages take work, but it's the best investment of time and energy you can ever make."

CRYSTAL *and* JASON

MARRIED 9 YEARS
OKLAHOMA CITY, OKLAHOMA

"At the age of 16, I moved from Long Beach, California to Moore, Oklahoma. It was slightly disappointing, to say the least. On my third day here, my aunt and uncle, took me to a mom-and-pop diner after church. Jason was our waiter. He had dreadlocks, piercings, and wore a hat of my favorite band. It was a little slice of home in the boring Midwest. He asked what I wanted to drink. I said, 'root beer' and that was about it. Two years later, I got a job at the same restaurant and Jason was still working there. I recognized him, but of course he didn't remember the 16-year-old girl who ordered a root beer two years prior. We quickly became friends. He talked about whatever book he was reading at the time and how books were so much better than relationships, while I talked about my dream life with a husband and kids."

"About a year later, my boyfriend broke up with me. I was completely heartbroken, because I was convinced he was 'the one.' I remember being so angry, and even praying that I didn't ever want to date again until I met my husband. Then, one day, Jason came up to me after his shift, totally clueless about my situation and said 'I don't know what's going on with you, but you're not really fun to work with lately. So, if you just need to talk or something, here's my phone number.'"

When he walked away, I got butterflies and then denied it for months. Hanging out, turned into making out, and the rest is history." After two years of dating, Crystal and Jason were married. They now have three children.

"Neither of us had a good example of marriage in our lives. We both came from broken families. We were actually terrified of getting married, because of the possibility of continuing that cycle. We finally determined that we loved each other enough, and trusted God enough, to say 'I Do,' and really mean it. We started from scratch, unlearning a lot of destructive behaviors and attitudes. We had no idea how to do marriage. We've struggled with learning how to really love and respect one another. I have had to grow from wanting to be in control of everything, to learning how to trust. Jason has had to grow from fear and passivity, to confidence and leadership. We both have had to learn how to communicate and resolve conflict. In fact, we are still learning this."

"The most helpful thing for us in our marriage has been to find older couples to mentor us. We've sought out couples that have been married for a long time, and have asked for their counsel and wisdom. It has been so encouraging to know we are not figuring it all out on our own."

"Marriage is such a mix of good and hard. It requires a commitment to do the hard things, to sacrifice for one another, and to make it great. We're not satisfied with just being committed to one another forever and to never leave. We want to build a legacy and fulfill our dreams together. We want our marriage and family to bring glory to God."

"Sometimes we get so caught up in the rest of life and doing our 'own thing,' whether it's jobs or to-do lists, or even taking care of our kids, that we forget that we're partners. We so easily turn our spouse into our enemy. Thankfulness has been our key to staying on the same team and enjoying one another."

As an inter-racial family, they have encountered some racism, which has created hard situations. "We don't think of ourselves as very different, because it is our normal. Our goal as a family is to love God and love others well… this extends to all people. In our first conversation about race identity with our five-year-old son, explaining that he was half black and half white, he exclaimed 'Wow, I get to be both?!?!' The perspective of a child is so great!"

"The definition of adventure is 'an unusual and exciting experience that requires risk.' We want our marriage to be exactly that. It is definitely unusual. There are no two people on this earth quite like us. We are uniquely, 'The Partees' and that is powerful. We don't have any idea what the future holds, but facing it together is fun and courageous. It is risky to commit our whole entire life to another person without a real guarantee of the outcome. This requires tons of faith and love. Marriage is an adventure and we are each other's greatest adventure."

"An amazing marriage to us is building a legacy, where we are glorifying God, being everything we were designed to be together." ♥

"We don't have any idea what the future holds, but facing it together is fun and courageous. It is risky to commit our whole entire life to another person without a real guarantee of the outcome. This requires tons of faith and love. Marriage is an adventure and we are each other's greatest adventure."

SARA *and* STEPHEN

MARRIED 6 YEARS
WEATHERFORD, OKLAHOMA

"Nothing of value comes easy. You have to be able to lean on each other. Don't feel like one person has to make all of the decisions or do everything. Lean on each other." ♥

SHELLY *and* SCOTT

MARRIED 26 YEARS
PORTLAND, OREGON

Shelly and Scott met in college at Pacific Lutheran University in Tacoma, Washington. "The first night we hung out, we danced around campus for about three hours and just talked. It was fun because I could be silly with him. Scott brought out that silly side of me."

They started dating in November of 1984 and continued through college. "Scott was very handsome. He was very quiet and kind of shy. But, when I got to know him, he was so fun and kind. He reminded me a lot of my dad. I kept seeing qualities of my dad in him, and that was a good thing to me."

Shelly and Scott were married in May, 1989. "We immediately moved to a tiny town in South Carolina for Scott's job in the lumber industry. We were there for six and a half years, and it challenged us. We struggled with infertility in those early years of marriage, as well as the typical struggles of newlyweds making a life together."

"We moved back to Oregon in 1995, and that is where we adopted our sweet baby boy, Jack. We witnessed the birth of our adopted son in March, 1997. The day of his birth was a long-awaited miracle for us. I'll never forget the joy of that day."

When Jack was seven months old, Scott was transferred to Ruston, Louisiana. "We were there for four and a half years and then off to Eagle, Idaho in another transfer. That is where our son was diagnosed as being on the autism spectrum. We lived in Idaho for three years and then after another transfer, Scott left his job so that we could live closer to family, and he wouldn't have to travel so much for his job. We've been 'home' a little over seven years and can see so many reasons why this is where we needed to be. We have amazing doctors and therapists for our son to thrive."

Infertility, adoption, and raising a child with special needs are three things that could rip a couple apart. Yet, Shelly and Scott are closer than ever. "We realized we make a great team and need each other. When one of us is having a hard day, the other steps in to fill the need. We couldn't do it alone."

This year, Shelly was diagnosed with Breast Cancer and recently started chemotherapy. "We are focusing on the 'in sickness and health' part of our vows. Dealing with cancer has been rough. But, again, it's brought us closer. I don't know how I would have gotten through the last four months without Scott. He has been my 'Steady Eddy' through every appointment, surgery, and procedure. I have always had strong faith and I have always known that Scott loves me. However, when the rubber hits the road and I have no hair, or I am throwing up from the chemo, I am even more grateful to know he is by my side every step of the way. He says I am beautiful even with my bald head, and he takes away all of those superficial fears I think are so important. He is there every step of the way on this scary journey."

"Everything is always changing. There are always new things coming into our lives and new challenges to deal with. Having to grow together and navigate that new path that we never thought we would be on, forces us to learn how to get through it together. We always think we are so strong, and then it happens to us. We are constantly learning about ourselves, and then about each other, and how we relate to each other. I don't think we ever stop learning, and growing, and becoming a better version of ourselves. I don't think we ever have it all figured out, or have found an equation for a perfect marriage. I don't think that ever happens."

"Last year we celebrated our 25th wedding anniversary with our families and a few close friends. We celebrated the challenges as well as the many joys, and the fact that we had survived the storms that wanted to ravage our marriage. We have learned over the years that even within marriage, things are still going to be up and down. There are going to be peaks and valleys, hard times and good times. We have rough patches and we have learned to stick it out."

"Our best advice for other couples is to remember your vows and what you said. They are not just words. You are really promising something to this person you are standing in front of. On the wedding day, we often think it is just this fairy tale. I can honestly say, I love Scott more today than the day we got married. I think it comes with all of the challenges we have been through together."

"My favorite thing about being married is that I have a partner to walk through this messy life alongside. We balance each other out, and I'd like to think we bring out one another's best. I honestly can't imagine life without him." ♥

"My favorite thing about being married is that I have a partner to walk through this messy life alongside."

MORGAN *and* RON

MARRIED 6 YEARS
PORTLAND, OREGON

"Know what lights your spouse up... and then remove every obstacle for them so that they can enjoy what lights them up! When we do that for each other, life is so much more fun. When Ron does that for me, I feel known and appreciated for who I am. I feel like we are sharing something that is really meaningful. Even though he doesn't do yoga and I don't rock climb, we can still be excited for the other person and make it easier for them to make time for those things. This is also something we teach our kids: be excited about what someone else is excited about. That is a way to show love." ♥

JANIE *and* WAYNE

MARRIED 62 YEARS
MONTOURSVILLE, PENNSYLVANIA

"On our first date we went to the movies. We had to take a bus, because he wasn't 16 yet." ♥

LOIS *and* MIKE

MARRIED 30 YEARS
NEW BERLIN, PENNSYLVANIA

"Trust who you are with and love who you are. You have to love yourself before you can love anybody else." ♥

CARIN *and* JAIME

MARRIED 12 YEARS
BLANDON, PENNSYLVANIA

Carin and Jaime met in college. They were in a Sociology class together, but actually didn't realize that until after they met one night at a bar called 'The Rat.' "Romantic huh? That is why I always tell people we met in Sociology class."

"It has been 15 years and I can still remember the exact moment I laid eyes on Jaime. Later that night his friend tried to hit on my friend, which didn't go over well. But Jaime and I hit it off and he walked me home that night. We talked until we fell asleep. He left his phone number on a slip of paper, and from that point on, we were together."

They both graduated, found jobs, and during the Summer of 2000 were engaged. Jaime asked Carin to marry him during a 4th of July picnic in front of her whole family.

At that point, Jaime had dedicated his life to public service. He was in the military and a police officer. Going into their relationship, they talked about the sacrifices they would have to make, but everything became a little more real on September 11, 2001.

"Without a doubt, September 11th was a defining moment for both of us, because we just didn't know what was going to happen. We had a wedding planned and we knew it was only a matter of time until Jaime

would be deployed. Everyone was in a state of precariousness."

Carin and Jaime were married one month after September 11, 2011, and just months later, Jaime left on his first deployment overseas.

"Newlyweds are supposed to spend their first year of marriage together building memories. Jaime and I spent that year writing letters and exchanging 'I love yous' over the phone thousands of miles away. I suffered a miscarriage soon after he left. Our first anniversary came and went, and he returned home later that Fall."

"We were finally together again, but not for long. We only had 56 days before his next deployment. Those 56 days were almost like a honeymoon. We didn't really have time to get into the nitty-gritty of life's routines."

Between the deployments, they bought their first home together and Carin became pregnant. Shortly after, Jaime was off to Iraq. "I was pregnant and moving into our first house. Man I was angry back then. I felt like we were being robbed of all these special 'first' moments that newlyweds have. Time we couldn't get back."

During that deployment, they did not have contact by phone. They were only able to communicate by letters. There was no connectivity. However, Jaime did get to come home to witness the birth of their daughter.

"I hadn't seen Jaime for months and then he came home and I was nine months pregnant. I was huge and had all kinds of hormones."

After just two weeks of being home and welcoming their daughter into their lives, Jaime was back on a plane to finish his second deployment. "Our second anniversary came and went, I spent the Fall with my mom, grandparents, and our newborn daughter. He came home Christmas Eve, and I can tell you, that it was the best Christmas ever. We were finally together and we had a beautiful daughter."

"He came home and it was like we were newlyweds again. We had spent two years apart and were starting over. But now, we had a new house and a baby. It was actually hard. Coming home is always the harder part of a deployment. I wish I could say that our marriage and our life was blissfully happy. It should have been. But the war in Iraq had changed Jaime. It had changed both of us. He came home and we now had a three-month-old baby. He wanted to come home to the honeymoon part of our marriage, and I was tired. I was raising a baby here by myself. Jaime was going through some rough times getting used to being a civilian again. He harbored a lot of resentment and anger towards the war and towards people who didn't have to go through it. We went through some very dark times where I think both of us questioned our marriage. We went to a couple of Army Strong Bond Retreats that really helped us take a step back and realize that these deployments changed both of us, and we needed to stop expecting the other person to revert back to how things were before he left. We had to learn to love each other again."

"Eleven years went by, new jobs, new houses, two more kids, and then the worst happened again, another deployment. This time to Afghanistan. I won't lie and say I wasn't scared. I knew what the other deployments did to our marriage. What if it happens again? And now we have three children. How will I survive a deployment AND take care of three kids who are equally scared?"

However, their third deployment taught them that the work they did to get through the other two deployments made their marriage stronger. "I can tell you that I am not scared for our marriage anymore. I am more certain than ever that our marriage is even stronger. Every text, every Skype call, every email, every phone call, our love grows even stronger. Jaime is my best friend, my partner, and my everything. Whatever the future throws at us, I know that we will conquer it together."

"Deployments are so stressful on both sides. They forced us to grow up a lot faster than our friends. When we got married, the army told us we needed to have a will and a power of attorney. It was an eye opener. We were like 'whoa, we just got married, and we are in our 20s.'"

"It is possible to get through the pain, regret, and bitterness. It takes patience and reaching out for help. There is a lot that happened during Jaime's deployment that I still do not know. I asked him once or twice, but he wouldn't answer. I was sad about that for quite awhile, because we were best friends, and then he stopped talking to me. It was frustrating to not have him communicating with me. But, by seeking help through the Army, we were reminded that we are all human. What was happening in our relationship was normal. We just needed to continue to communicate and talk."

"Our biggest hope is that we can reach out to some of these younger couples who are on their first or second deployments and give them hope. I can definitely say today that I have the marriage I dreamed of. It isn't all rainbows and unicorns every day. But, I know that now, we can get through just about anything because we have each other."

"An amazing marriage is having fun together. Every day is an adventure that we know we want to go on together." ♥

"It isn't all rainbows and unicorns every day. But, I know that now, we can get through just about anything because we have each other."

CINDY *and* JERRY

MARRIED 44 YEARS
ELIZABETHTOWN, PENNSYLVANIA

"During our first couple of years of being married, we didn't have a whole lot of money. That probably molded our view of what we needed in life to be happy." ♥

MARY ELLEN *and* ALLEN

MARRIED 64 YEARS
SHAMOKIN DAM, PENNSYLVANIA

"I am one that really can say, behind every successful man, there is a brilliant woman. I will tell anybody that."

"I think I had all D's during my first semester at Lycoming College. I got called in by the Dean, and he asked me if college was right for me. So, I went home and told Mary Ellen. She got her temper up and said, 'We'll show him.' My senior year, I made the Dean's List."

"She drove me and helped me get through. I would go hunting instead of going to classes. But, she was after me, and that was one of the best things that ever happened. I never really realized how much that meant to me." ♥

GRACE *and* TODD

MARRIED 8 YEARS
EAST PROVIDENCE, RHODE ISLAND

"Grace and I met at Summer Camp when I was 15 years old and she was 13 years old. She was so much different than anyone I had met before. She seemed to care about things in life that mattered far more than typical high school worries."

Despite living 50 miles from each other, Grace and Todd started dating when she was 15 years old and he was 17 years old. "We came of age loving one another."

A few years down the road, Todd realized a dream of touring the country as a musician. The distance added stress on their relationship and they decided to part ways.

"We both felt confident that we wanted to spend our lives together, but we just didn't understand how to handle the different directions our lives were taking at the time. It was really complicated, because we were so emotionally serious at such a young age. It was very messy and confusing. I really missed him, because we grew up together. He felt like family to me, more so than a best friend."

After spending a year apart, growing as individuals, Grace and Todd came back together as new people and rekindled a great love based on where they were headed together, instead of where they had come. "Where we ended up, was a relationship between two different people with shared histories."

"I don't look back fondly on the time apart, but I see the character it produced, and I see the fruit knowing that is what life is about. Our young age, searching for our own identities, and baggage from emotional confusion, were all very difficult to manage. However, in reuniting we realized that it was patience, understanding, and hope in redemption of lost and broken things, that our relationship had become a testament. It has become the platform on which we exist, and the way we see our future together far beyond all empty horizons before us."

"We were married in 2007, on a beautiful New England Summer day, and have since settled a home in Providence, Rhode Island with our dog Ollie, and two children, August and Ayla Mae."

"Now that we are in our early 30s, we are like an old married couple (in a good way), because we have already been through so much together and feel like we can really last through anything."

"One of my favorite things about being married is how we complement each other so well. I can slow him down and he can pick me up. That is the beauty of it. I would be imbalanced without

him, in the way that I felt imbalanced when we were apart during our breakup in our early twenties."

"The most exciting thing we have been through, and continue to go through together, is welcoming our children into our lives. Both the birth of our daughter and son, and also the passing seasons, have taught us to appreciate moments more fully and to work together more."

"I would love our kids to see in us what we have seen in our parents who have each been married for 40+ years. A relationship, especially marriage, is about the commitment and seeing each other through the ups, downs, and changes. When you are married for 40 years, you are going to be totally different people from ages 20-60. I would just love for our kids to learn to be brave and courageous enough to stick it out with the person they are committed to, knowing they will see the joy and the fruit in it."

"The opportunity of marriage is not guaranteed. It is very fragile and needs to be fed and cared for and invested in. We've realized that in some tougher times when we haven't invested in it, and we've seen the benefit in other times when we have."

"Our secret to a happy marriage is to learn from those who have been at it for longer than us. Life is hard and you just can't do it alone."

"An amazing marriage is one that grows. It is never finished." ♥

"Life is hard and you just can't do it alone."

EMILY *and* MICHAEL

MARRIED 3 YEARS
CHARLESTON, SOUTH CAROLINA

Emily and Michael met while attending the College of Charleston. They met through a mutual friend during Emily's first year and Michael's senior year of college. They started dating in April, and Michael graduated in May. They both stayed in Charleston that Summer to be able to hang out with one another. Eventually, Michael went to Law School in Columbia, about two hours from Charleston. They dated long-distance for the next three years. Michael moved back to Charleston, and about three months later, he helped Emily move to Columbia so she could attend Graduate School.

In February 2012, Michael proposed to Emily.

"We were married a few months later on an unseasonably warm November day in a tiny, country church packed with our friends and family. I was 30 minutes late to the wedding and we forgot to sign the marriage license, but it was an amazingly beautiful day, and we both agree, it was the best day of our lives so far."

At the time they were married, Emily and Michael were still living 90 miles apart. Their careers and job opportunities at the time made sense for them to live separately. "*It seems kind of cold now, but it made so much sense at the time. We kind of got used to it. What is another year after dating for so many years long-distance?*"

"It didn't feel as difficult until after we were married. I don't know if that was outside pressure or pressure we were putting on ourselves."

"When we got married, we wanted to start our lives together and share all of these experiences in our first year of marriage. We felt like we were missing out on each other. We wanted more than being apart. It was fine when we were dating, but when we were married, we wanted more fulfillment from our relationship. It was difficult to get that when we had to FaceTime or talk on the phone whenever we wanted to talk."

"I think it is good to compare your relationship to other people who have established and healthy relationships as a benchmark. But, I think that constant comparison is something that our generation does because we have Facebook and Instagram, and see it everywhere. I think that is a bad road to go down. Everyone has their own relationship. Everyone moves at their own pace. When we first got married, it was really hard for me to see my other friends who were getting married, buying a house, decorating their house, and having babies, while we were still stuck in separate cities. It was hard for me. I just had to take a step back and realize that everyone has their own journey."

Eventually, Emily received a call from a recruiter and accepted a job in Charleston. They have lived together for two years and recently purchased their first home together. "It's crazy how much can happen in just three years. This year has been exciting for us because we bought this house, and we are making it our home."

"Through so many years in a long-distance relationship, we realized that it doesn't matter where we are, as long as we are together. I would never want to do that again. We did it, and I think we are stronger for it. But, I wouldn't want to have to redo that. Being apart made us really appreciate the time we have together, even if we're just lying in bed reading, or on the couch watching a movie. Our time is better together."

"We do our best to appreciate everything, even the difficult conversations. We appreciate that we have a person to have those discussions with. We are fortunate that we get to do that. We are fortunate to have each other and grow together."

An amazing marriage is one that can adapt to change and be stronger for it. Situations change and people change over time. Lasting love is love that is strong enough to adapt and continue to grow through change." ♥

TAMMY *and* BRIAN

MARRIED 4 MONTHS
SIOUX FALLS, SOUTH DAKOTA

On a night in February 2013, Tammy received a text from a number that said he had received her number from Tammy's friend. Tammy was initially intrigued because he had a Nebraska phone number, which is where she grew up.

"What I didn't know was that he was in Mississippi, about to deploy a month later." Tammy and Brian started chatting daily, but didn't meet for seven months. "We just talked and FaceTimed. There was a big time difference, but we talked everyday."

"I missed him, but I didn't even know him. It was more of a friendship during those seven months."

Four days after getting back from deployment, Brian went to Sioux Falls, South Dakota to meet Tammy. "I remember seeing him coming around the corner and I ran upstairs because I was so nervous. But, we talked that evening like we had known each other forever."

Both Tammy and Brian had been married before and Tammy has two children from her previous marriage. It was important to them not to bring the children into their relationship until they knew there was something extra special. Tammy and Brian started dating in September, and introduced Brian to the children in January. Just over a year later, they were married. "It was a mutual decision. I chose to marry Brian and he chose to marry me. Our wedding day was about

us and our marriage, not about having a party for our friends and family."

"Being our second marriages, we have a better understanding of what we are looking for. I know what it actually means to get married, compared to my first marriage when I was 22 years old. I asked Brian questions that I didn't ask in my first marriage. I didn't know to ask those questions at 21 years old. We talked about our core values before we even met each other face-to-face, because I wanted to make sure we were on the same page. I needed him to know things upfront."

"Communication, trust, and sex are the three things that we think are most important in a relationship. When one of them is missing, we know something is going to fall off. Communication has always been a work in progress for us. Brian was in the military and everything is very black and white for him. I am more flowery and emotional. I tend to be very sensitive, too. He could say something, and I could spin it into something negative so quickly, even though he didn't mean it that way. We have decided that every time we read a text, we read it with a positive tone."

"We both learned a lot from our first marriages. Even if they failed, we learned something. Because of that, I felt like we both came into our marriage with a willingness to make it work, because we know what it feels like when it doesn't. Love is a choice. I choose to love him every morning."

"Having someone to share moments with and go on adventures with is my favorite thing about being married. I hiked by myself for a long time. It is way more fun to share that experience with Brian."

An amazing marriage to us is one with no regrets." ♥

"Love is a choice.
I choose to love him every morning."

BAILEY *and* JOSH

MARRIED 2 WEEKS
SIOUX FALLS, SOUTH DAKOTA

"An amazing marriage is two best friends supporting each other." ♥

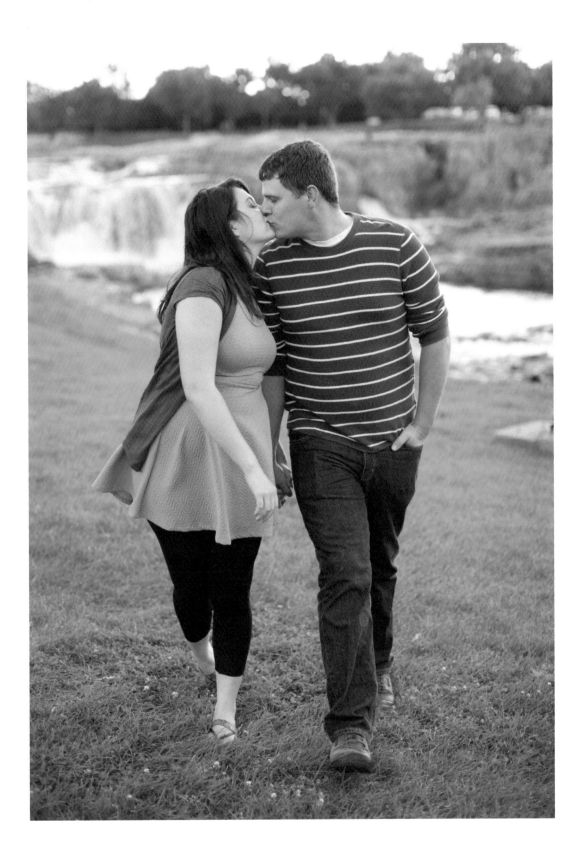

NICOLE *and* TYLER

MARRIED 1 YEAR
MEMPHIS, TENNESSEE

"I met Tyler when I was a sophomore in high school. I had never dated anyone, but had a crush on this guy I always told my Mom was 'kind of cute.' Tyler was a senior baseball player. We never spoke more than a few words to one another before he moved off to college. I continued through my last two years of high school. The summer before my senior year, Tyler, this boy that was 'kind of cute,' randomly showed interest in me. We casually dated from September through March of my senior year, and got serious April of 2009."

Nicole and Tyler dated for three years before getting engaged. "*We got engaged the summer of 2012. That was the summer after I graduated from college. I got my first full-time job that June, and I thought 'Oh I got a job now; I'll buy a car; and ask her to marry me.'*" Nicole and Tyler were married the following March.

"We went into our marriage knowing that marriage is a covenant, not a contract. Love is not something that you just feel. We made a covenant and we believe it's supposed to look like how Christ has a covenant with His church. When things get hard, there is no getting out, there is getting through. I think that has helped us look at problems and situations knowing that we are in this no matter what. A contract can be voided if one person doesn't hold up their end of the deal. But a covenant means if one person does not hold up their end of the deal, the other

will stay true to who he/she is supposed to be. Recognizing that difference has clarified the way we look at our marriage and the purpose of it."

"I don't look for Tyler to fulfill every desire that I have, because I'm not made for him to fulfill every desire that I have. We weren't made to be completely fulfilled by each other."

"We have learned to not expect perfection. We take every day as it comes; enjoy it; love it; and when things go wrong, we know that it's going to be okay. There are going to be days that we fight or something doesn't happen the way we want. But, that's okay. Everybody has days or moments."

"*I really thought it was going to be a strange adjustment to live with somebody, but it was just kind of fun to have one of my best friends to hang out with all the time. We got to hang out every day, be with each other, and have dinner together. It was really a fun time to discover some new things about each other that we didn't know before.*"

"In our first six months of marriage, my sweet little world of being together every day stopped for about six months because Tyler had to train for a job in Nashville. That was hard. I was a mess until he left. I had severe anxiety. I cried every day. But once we got used to it, it opened up a lot of opportunities. The Lord opened all

kinds of doors that I wouldn't have been open to if I had Tyler home every day. It really stretched us a lot."

"The biggest obstacle we have faced in our marriage is our own selves. Marriage is such a selfless thing. I have to put him first, apologize first, initiate first, love first, and serve first. As a selfish human being, that is hard. But, what a JOY when we get it right from time to time!"

"The most exciting thing we've been through together has been starting our business together. While we were on our honeymoon, we took a million different video clips of our resort, our dinners, and our random adventures. Towards the end of our trip, Tyler said, 'Wouldn't it be fun if we got to do this all the time?' I remember laughing and saying 'Yeah, that's not going to happen!' I've lived a very 'in the box' life, but oh, how the Lord has used Tyler to pull me right out of it. We started our videography and photography company in August of 2013. God is so good and I'm so thankful He allows me to do life with Tyler every single day."

"Our marriage is amazing because I get to be on a mission with someone every day. Whether it's directly on mission for our faith, or on mission for our family, or on mission for our business, we live unified. We are together. I have a person, every day." ♥

"When things get hard,
there is no getting out,
there is getting through."

JESSICA *and* ERIC

MARRIED 14 YEARS
AUSTIN, TEXAS

"My friend from high school went to the Naval Academy and invited me to be his date at the International Ball during his sophomore year. I got all dressed up fancy, with my tiara and sparkly gown. I was on the dance floor when a big, clumsy, football player came across the ballroom on his way to the restroom and knocked me over onto the ground. At that point, Enrique Iglesias's *Will you be my Hero* was playing, and he reached down to ask me to dance. That was it. We danced the rest of the night together."

"At that time, I was working at Disney World and had just auditioned for Cinderella. I did not get the role. But, while I was dancing with Eric, I couldn't stop thinking, 'I am at a Ball; there is a boy in uniform; and it's love at first sight. I have my very own Cinderella Story.'"

"*It wasn't as fairy tale for me, but I was definitely still very excited about it.*"

Just a few weeks later, Eric flew down to Florida to meet Jessica at Disney World. They continued to date long-distance, seeing each other about once per month.

"The long-distance helped our relationship, because we talked on the phone for hours. We truly got to know each other on a mental level."

Eric proposed to Jessica in front of Cinderella's Castle on July 4, 2003. Jessica graduated early from Texas A&M and moved to Annapolis, Maryland to be closer to Eric during his senior year. They planned their wedding for June 2004, just two weeks after Eric's graduation.

"*We got married and did our honeymoon, and then that is where the fairy tale ended. I went to training for the Marine Corps. It was a repeat of our dating life, because*"

I was almost never around."

In 2006, Eric received orders for deployment in Iraq. He left three days later.

"I was 24 years old at the time and just having fun in Orange County, trying not to think about the deployment. Fortunately, I lived near Eric's family and my best friend moved to California to live with me during that time. She was there for me. Every Thursday she had off work, and we went to Disney Land. That was my happy place. I stayed busy."

Jessica and Eric's communication was very limited during the deployment. "We videotaped ourselves, burned it to a disk, and mailed it to each other. Occasionally, Eric had the chance to call me, so I literally lived with my phone that year."

After returning home nine months later, Eric received new orders for a second deployment.

"The second deployment was much harder for me. He had just made it home safely and then we had to do it all again. I still remember him calling me to tell me about the orders. I was in Texas at the time. He said, 'I have an opportunity to lead a platoon, but I won't do it if you don't want me to. However, it is everything I have ever wanted in my life. It is everything I have been training for. I have to leave again this month, and I will be gone another year.' I was devastated."

Eric left for training and his second deployment just one month after returning home from his first deployment.

"One of the weird things about leaving and coming back from this deployment was how quickly it all happened. When I left, everything *was setup in our house in Orange County. While I was deployed, Jessica decided to move home with her parents, so she put everything into storage. When I came back, she had found another house in a different city and moved everything in. So, when I got home, everything was setup and it was a whole new house."*

"It was important to me for Eric to come home to a house, and not have us wondering where we were going next."

"It did make it a lot easier."

"I almost feel like I was in a bubble the first five years of marriage, just surviving deployment to deployment. We moved six times in four years. I focused on the logistics of making it all work. Being an independent woman was definitely the key for me as a military wife."

Eric's next orders were for a more "regular job with almost normal hours" in Bakersfield, California.

"Leaving and coming back so much, we had all of these happy reunions where we were excited to see each other. Then, we started seeing each other every day. It was an adjustment to get used to being around one another."

"It's learning. Every step of marriage is a new adventure."

"While Eric was on his first deployment, we both made a list separately of 100 things we wanted to do in our lives. We mailed them to each other and a lot of them ended up being travel related. We don't have a lot in common, but we do have a love of adventure in common. At that time, we decided someday we were going to take a trip around the world. We spent the next seven years planning that trip. That was at the forefront of all of our decisions. We even held off having a family, so we could go on this trip."

In 2013, Jessica and Eric sold their home in Bakersfield and backpacked around the world. "That trip was a big turning point of really getting to know one another again."

Since that trip around the world, Jessica and Eric moved to Austin, Texas and welcomed their son, Evan into their lives.

One thing Jessica and Eric learned very early on in their relationship is the importance of their individuality and taking time for themselves. "I know we need time apart. I go on trips and Eric goes on trips. We get that time to refresh and then come back together. I think that was a pattern from day one of meeting each other."

"Marriage is a roller coaster, and it is not always a fairy tale. I was very naïve early on in our relationship, that I had found my Prince Charming and it was a Cinderella story. That fairy tale fades very quickly if you don't have a base of respect for each other. The hard times do come and when they do, we rely on our foundation of respect and communication. We are still working on that, even 12 years into our marriage. It's a roller coaster. Brace yourself and build a foundation of love and respect. That goes a long way."

"An amazing marriage is full of adventure, joy, and respect." ♥

"Marriage is a roller coaster, and it is not always a fairy tale. I was very naïve early on in our relationship, that I had found my Prince Charming and it was a Cinderella story. That fairy tale fades very quickly if you don't have a base of respect for each other."

SHIREEN *and* NICK

MARRIED 11 YEARS
SALT LAKE CITY, UTAH

"Shireen and I met in the fall of 1999 at St. Cloud State University in St. Cloud, Minnesota. Brenda Weiler, a North Dakota folk musician, played a show on campus during the first few weeks of our freshmen year. Afterwards, I took one of the show posters as a souvenir. It's a pink poster covered in pastel colored flowers with a woman holding a guitar in the center. In other words, it's not very 'manly' and I debated whether or not to hang it. Thankfully I did, because a couple days later, a bespectacled, curly haired woman stopped by to ask about the owner of that poster. That's how we met."

"In 2003, during our senior year, we applied for the Peace Corps. The application required us to check our marital status. We checked 'engaged,' though we were not. Low and behold, we were accepted. The catch was that we had to be married by the time we left. We finished our undergraduate degrees in May, married in August, and left for the Republic of Moldova in September. It was a difficult and incredible experience, and I'm glad we shared it together."

Shireen and Nick returned to the United States in 2005. Nick began working in television news and Shireen continued her studies. They moved roughly every other year and eventually ended up in Utah.

"I have always loved work. I loved the pride that came with the responsibility of selling sweet corn when I was 14 years old, bagging groceries when I was 15 years old, slinging coffee through college, and every news job I've had. I've always identified with what I've done for work. After a couple news jobs, I took a marketing job that I thought was a dream job. It paid well. It had regular work hours, something I've never had with news. However, the job made me miserable for all the reasons jobs make people miserable: unsatisfying work, bad boss, and days that dragged on and on. I brought a lot of this frustration home with me and it affected our marriage."

"I had in my head the whole time that I would decide if our marriage ended or not. It never crossed my mind that the way I was acting might make Shireen not want to be married to me. I was in this crazy fog. However, once I accepted that my job was the source of the boredom that was festering into other problems, I decided a better paying job was not worth pushing people away. So, I quit. And I returned to my passion, which is daily news."

"I feel like marriage is something we work at. There are things about marriage that are difficult, and there are things about it that are great. We are committed to it and fulfilled by the investment that we make. Marriage is something we have worked at, continue to work at, and will continue to work at. That's why it is what it is. I'm proud of that. We believe that individual

growth doesn't end with marriage. Continuing to grow as individuals is what feeds growth as a couple. It keeps things interesting and dynamic. It has been important for us to maintain hobbies and friends that are ours. It makes those porch conversations more interesting."

"We are going to be different people in a year, than we are now. We are really different people than we were when we got married. We've been lucky that we've been able to grow and change, and it's still something that we want to be a part of. In marriage, you take that risk. You choose to be up for the potential of who your spouse is and who that person might become. Being aware that the person you marry on your wedding day is not the person that you will die with is so important. We all change. And that's actually a really exciting prospect, but it does involve having faith in that person. The reality is, the Shireen that I married, wouldn't interest me today. And hopefully, Shireen at 50 years old would say that she is not interested in who I was at 35 years old."

"The most exciting thing about our marriage is that we've built something that is not built on exciting moments. It's built on enjoying the steady everydayness of our life together. I have found my day to day with Shireen to be the most exciting: beers on the porch at night, picking out colors to paint the bedrooms, and conversations on long car rides across Nebraska."

"I think we grow up with this idea that our wedding day is going to be the most important day of our lives. I don't think it is good to be married to an idea of how something will be. Our wedding was great. However, I think if I would have been thinking about my wedding my whole life, I probably would have been disappointed. It wasn't this huge thing. I found my dress on a sales rack at The Limited."

"There is no perfect, right? There's no normal, and there's no perfect. Whatever you're doing, if you can make it work, that's great. Don't put yourself in this trap of expecting this gorgeous wedding day, huge wedding, nonstop happiness, and then nonstop children, or whatever it is you are expecting. There is no right way to do life. There are a lot of right ways to do life."

"The Peace Corps has given me this perspective: We have won the jackpot being born in this country and having the opportunities that we've had. A lot of those opportunities have come to us in pretty easy ways. To think that if the hardest thing that happens to us is Nick hating his jobs and wanting to end our marriage for a period of time, that's like a breeze. We've had to deal with almost nothing in the grand scheme of things."

"Our marriage is amazing because it's hilarious and there's also an element of the absurd." ♥

"I feel like marriage is something we work at. There are things about marriage that are difficult and there are things about it that are great. We are committed to it and fulfilled by the investment that we make. Marriage is something we have worked at, continue to work at, and will continue to work at. That's why it is what it is. I'm proud of that."

DENISE *and* BILL

MARRIED 17 YEARS
SEARSBURG, VERMONT

"We met during the summer while working at the White House of Wilmington, a small Inn. Bill was working in maintenance and I was a housekeeper. I was cleaning a room when I looked out the window and saw Bill with his long hair, ripped jeans, and his earing. I immediately said 'Who is that? He is really cute.' And the woman I was with said, 'oh that's Billy, he is trouble. Stay away from him.'"

That didn't stop Denise. She was so attracted to Bill, she picked him up at the bar. "The tragic part of that, is that I thought he was just like every other guy who had used me in the past."

But Bill had other plans and was not ready to just walk away. They fell in love with one another, dated on and off, and fought through trust issues.

"It's a messy story. It definitely was not a fairy tale. I was at the lowest point in my life when I met him. When I look back on it, Bill was like an angel coming into my life. God definitely put us together at that time. We both grew up in alcoholic homes, so we had very bad education on relationships."

During a period where Denise and Bill were not dating, Denise had moved out to Wisconsin. "Bill came out to see me. We were riding in his car and we were arguing. I remember saying, I wish someone gave us a manual about relationships. You get a manual for your microwave and your washing machine and your fridge, why don't you get a manual about relationships? Little did we know, there is a manual, the Bible. But at the time, we didn't realize that. We were so wanting someone to just tell us how to do this."

There was a period of four or five years where Denise and Bill lost contact and did not see one another. "In that time, I got married and got separated. I went and tried to find someone who was the exact opposite of Bill. That did not work well. I was just running. In that same time, Bill dated a girl for a very brief time and she got pregnant."

"My heart just went through the floor when Bill told me he had a child on the way. I literally prayed to get him out of my heart."

One day, Bill showed up at Denise's home with a gift of a Bible. During that same time, he asked one of Denise's neighbor's to share the Gospel with her. Denise dove in and started growing as a person.

"We started talking and seeing each other then. We really felt like God wanted us to be together. After all of this time, we were both kind of like 'No God, we really don't think that is a good idea. We have a bad history together.'"

"There was no doubt about it that it was a God thing. We had been through so much. Individually, previously through our relationships, and then in our relationship, we had been through a lot of hurt and pain."

"It was definitely way different this time because we had a spiritual aspect that we had never had before. And we had the manual."

"During the Fall of 1997, I drove to Wilmington to have dinner with Bill. God was speaking to me and said, 'you are exactly where you are suppose to be.' As I drove up there, this peace came over me, and God told me, 'He can't be the man I've called him to be without you.'"

Bill proposed to Denise that night. "It was a complete surprise to me, but God told me I was exactly where I was suppose to be."

After 13 years of dating off and on, Denise and Bill were married in January, 1998.

"Even now, it doesn't matter what life looks like, I know in the deepest part of my being that I am where I am suppose to be, and he is where he is suppose to be. It doesn't matter how messy it gets. Until God tells me something different, I am not going anywhere. It doesn't matter what life looks like."

"We are like two pieces of bread, and God is the Peanut Butter that holds us together."

"Nothing is impossible with God. Everything is possible. When we are having a hard time, I try to remember that Bill was made in the image of God. I should speak life into him. When I speak life into Bill and into our marriage, things change. Love is a decision that I make, not a feeling. Love takes courage to face our fears and insecurities."

"*What I love most about Denise is more of a knowing that we are meant to be together. I feel like the magnificence of our marriage is still to be. We came from such a broken place that we are not there yet. We have this amazing love for each other, but it is so mixed up by all of this mess we learned as children. We both have more healing that needs to happen, and we are together to help each other through that.*"

"Love endures all things and love never fails. It is bigger than us. It has been a powerful force in our lives. We have come through so much. I know that we are going to have good days ahead. Every day we work on it. The best is yet to come."

"It's hard and it's messy. But you can come from a broken place and still have an amazingly successful marriage." ♥

" It's hard and it's messy.
But, you can come from a
broken place and still have an
amazingly successful marriage."

AMBER *and* BRANDON

MARRIED 4 YEARS
HENRICO, VIRGINIA

Amber and Brandon met in fourth grade when Amber started going to Brandon's school. "As we got to know each other, he became my boyfriend in sixth grade. Our first date was on my birthday and Brandon's mom took us to Arby's. She even went across the street so that we could be alone. We were in love for a few months, but broke it off as you do in middle school."

Six years later, Amber and Brandon reconnected and started dating.

"In the beginning, we were both a bit selfish and I don't think we made each other a true priority. After a few times hurting each other's feelings, we really started talking about if we wanted this to work, or if it was going to be another dating fail. We decided we both wanted it and wanted to work on it. We chose to put each other as a priority in our lives. We chose to stand together through the tough times of lost loved ones, financial hurdles, job changes, and lots of other life stresses that got thrown at us."

After dating for about six years, Amber and Brandon were married. "Even though I know we are supported by our family and friends, it is always a good reminder to see it visually. Our wedding was a good testament to how much we are so loved and supported."

Knowing they wanted to have children right away, Amber had a conversation with her doctor and was told it would be very hard for her to conceive. "Being told that I could potentially not have children took a big toll on us. Very early on, we had to decide how much of our financial resources and emotional turmoil we were going to put ourselves through. It wasn't easy; in fact it was extremely hard. I was on medicines that made me a bit crazy, on top of being stressed out thinking I could maybe never be a Mama. It caused little fights between us."

"It took a long road of six fertility treatments before I found out on the Friday before Father's Day, in 2012, that we were going to have our very first baby. It was a trying time for our marriage. Every failure brought us closer and closer together, and every success meant we were one step closer to building a beautiful life together."

"In 2013, we welcomed our son, Nolan, to our family. Becoming a parent is definitely the most exciting thing we have ever done together. I really think seeing each other become parents made us love each other more and more."

"One of the things that has really kept our marriage strong is understanding each other and letting each other vent in the way that helps us in moving forward. We don't get bent out of shape, or take things too seriously, when we are in a vulnerable state."

"We have surrounded ourselves with a very

close-knit group of friends. All of our friends are married with children of their own, and we are all genuinely best friends. This helps us get out, but yet still spend time together. It also allows us to get advice and share stories from trusted friends that we know really understand what we are experiencing."

"Before getting married, we came to an understanding that this marriage is forever, and no matter how rocky it gets, we will get through it. We understand that 'getting through it' isn't just going to happen. It takes work on both ends."

"To say our marriage is perfect, would be the biggest joke. But to say we continually work on it, would be hitting the nail on the head!" ♥

MICHELE *and* STEVE

MARRIED 48 YEARS
GRAPEVIEW, WASHINGTON

"I had been in the United States for a week as an exchange student in the Hecht residence. Steve was coming home from Europe that day and I was swimming with Nancy, Steve's sister."

"*When I heard we were having a French girl come, the image in my head was a tall brunette. When I got there, she was a short blond. But, she did have a two-piece bathing suit on, and I was very interested.*"

"We got to know each other at his parent's house around the dining room table. We played a lot of ping-pong in his basement. I was teaching him all of the swear words in French, because I was always the one losing."

About two weeks after they met, Steve left for college. They corresponded by letters and phone calls. "*I have a very clear memory of my mother standing at the top of the steps in our big*

ol' three story house saying to me, 'why don't you ask Michele out on a date?' and I said, 'I am working on it, Mom.'"

"In those days, the boys always asked the girls out. I always say, he probably wouldn't have asked me out if he had to pick up the phone and call me. But, this way, he only had to ask me across the dining room table. So that was easy."

Around Christmas time of that year, Michelle and Steve went on a family trip to the Poconos. During that trip, they became more romantically involved. After Steve went back to college, he often received rides from his friends who would drive him six hours back to visit Michele. They continued dating with frequent visits from Steve.

"I left in June to go back to France and by then, we were fairly involved. It was during the Vietnam War. I remember thinking, 'This is too complicated. I am Catholic; he is Jewish. I am French; he is American. How are we going to work this out?'"

Because of the Vietnam War, there was no option for Steve to go to France with Michele.

"My intention was to go back to France to go to Sailing School and Law School. My idea was not to come back to the States, but he prevailed."

Michele had been on a student visa that expired, and the law at the time required her to stay out of the United States for two years. They were not planning to get married that young, but it was the only way they could be together.

Steve went over to France that Christmas to ask Michele's father formally for her hand in marriage. They got engaged. He was there for three weeks, and then he left to go back to

school. "We ended up planning our wedding from afar. My parents didn't have a phone at the time. So, when Steve wanted to call, he would call the priest's house that was two doors down the street, and then the priest would have to come and get me."

"I was moving to another country. I had so many things that I wanted to do in France, but they were inconsequential in the long run. It became a blur. I am a big believer that you just do it and things usually happen and fall into place. They work if you keep doing it. It is always a matter of moving forward, instead of saying, 'I can't do this.'"

It took about eight months to figure out all of the paperwork that was needed for Michele and Steve to officially be married and able to come back to the United States. They were married in August, with an official ceremony by the Mayor at City Hall, and then they had a church wedding and reception a few days later. After a three-week honeymoon in France, Steve came back to the States while Michele finished packing. As soon as she received her visa, they started their lives together in Philadelphia.

"I got pregnant very early on and that pretty much changed our lives. Steve stopped school to go to work with his father, and we moved to Baltimore. We were young. Our son, Eric, was a great kid and very easy baby. When he was two years old, he contracted a very bad infection. On a Monday, he was on antibiotics and he died that following Sunday morning."

"It was a pretty impossible time. For eight days, people were coming to the house. It became a blur. I understand now, but I didn't like it then. I had never been to a Jewish funeral. I had no clue what was expected. Everybody was there talking to us. The funerals we had at home in France were always very calm. It was not at all like that. There were lots of people around."

"I think going through that, reinforced our marriage. We were best friends. We needed each other and clung to each other."

"We tried to get pregnant right away to replace Eric. I was a mother and I wanted to continue to be a mother right away. We tried to adopt, but they wouldn't let us, because they told us we needed to grieve first. We ended up getting pregnant right away. After that, life settled. We bought our first house and that is where our three kids grew up."

"Marriage is pretty deep. I think people try to make it too hard and too perfect. We have to just let people be. We have to let the other person be their own and blossom on their own and together."

After spending most of their married lives together in Baltimore, Maryland, Michele and Steve sold their house and made the cross-country move closer to their grandchildren in Washington. "Thinking about the last years in our lives, the one thing we can leave behind is our family. If we want to teach at all, we must teach by example. We are very blessed to have three kids and four wonderful grandchildren that we get to see often. Plus, we are having fun!"

"When we moved into our home in Washington, we had a mess in the garage and a mess in the house. Guess what, we went out and bought two kayaks and went kayaking."

"Although marriage is a constant job and a work in progress, we would wish our kind of marriage on anybody." ♥

"Marriage is pretty deep. I think people try to make it too hard and too perfect. We have to just let people be. We have to let the other person be their own and blossom on their own and together."

LAURA *and* COLIN

MARRIED 4 YEARS
WASHINGTON, D.C.

"I was helping a friend move and she gave me a statue of a saint. She said that if I placed it near my bed, upside down, the saint would find me a husband. That night, we went out, and I met Colin."

The friend that Laura was helping move was also friends with Colin. She introduced them that night at a bar in Adams Morgan. Laura, who is Catalan and grew up in Barcelona, made a first impression on Colin with her knowledge of soccer.

"*I remember walking out of the bar that night thinking to myself, 'did I just meet my future wife?'*"

After three years of dating, Colin proposed while sitting by the creek at Rock Creek Park in D.C. They were married a year later with a legal ceremony at the Courthouse and then a small wedding celebration a few weeks later.

"*My favorite moment of our marriage so far was the day we got legally married. It was just the two of us. There was no audience. In that moment, it really was just the two of us. I just remember feeling very content and happy, thinking this is a very solid thing that will last going forward. I feel very fortunate to have that.*"

"I lost my mom when I was very young, and since then, I have felt lonely in this world. Being married to Colin means having my best friend next to me every day, knowing he has my back, and that I can count on him. Life is better when you have a good teammate to share it with. He is my best friend and is home to me."

"Home is where the heart is. It is true. I would love to be home and in Spain. But, I am always a little bit home with Colin. Every night when Colin holds me, I tell him. 'You hold me and everything is fine.' When I am in his arms, everything quiets down and I am okay. It's the place where I feel the safest. When I am happy and excited, and when I just need the world to disappear, having him hold me is how I have gotten through everything that we have gone through together. Having that, I feel very lucky."

"I am a pediatric physical therapist and love being around kids, so I was really excited to start a family with Colin. We negotiated before we got married to when we would start trying and compromised to wait a year. Unfortunately, months went by and getting pregnant wasn't happening for us. A year after trying, we started testing and we were diagnosed with unexplained infertility. Infertility is probably the biggest challenge we have faced together, adding frustration, sadness, and a lot of stress to our home."

"I got anxious right away. I started going to acupuncture and found a therapist. I wanted to try to deal with it in a positive way. I wanted to make sure that it did not rule our lives. I didn't want it to be the only thing I could think about for what I thought would be months, and has ended up being years of our lives."

Laura and Colin went through three rounds of IUIs before moving onto IVF. "We had our first egg retrieval that resulted in a good number of eggs. We were very excited, and then the next morning they called us to tell us that none of them turned into embryos. I remember that call. I remember exactly where I was and exactly what she said. My world just collapsed."

After doing a rescue ICSI, they ended up with one embryo. Laura and Colin called him Uno. "We miscarried Uno before we even knew I was pregnant. We had to start over and we had nothing left."

Laura and Colin went on a trip they had been planning to China, Japan, and Hawaii. When they returned to D.C., they did a second IVF treatment that unfortunately resulted in another miscarriage.

"The best way of describing fertility treatments, is a roller coaster. You go from the excitement of 'this is going great' to the 'no, this is not going to happen.'"

"Infertility is so hush hush. People just don't talk about it, even the miscarriages. If you lose your brother, or your sister, or your parents, you say it. When you lose your baby, no one really talks about it. So, when you do say it, people just don't know how to react or support you. It is challenging."

"For Laura, it was an incredibly personal thing. For me, I just felt like I am more on the sideline. The toughest thing for me was just watching her *deal with it. I know I just had to try to be a support to her and have the confidence that it will work."*

"For the guys, it's a concept, and for us, it is physical. So much of it is so theoretical for a male. For women who are going through it, it is physically painful and very uncomfortable. It just puts us in different fields."

"Looking back, it's been a really, really rough year, but I would not change any of it. I have learned so much about myself, and it has made us stronger as a couple. We are going to be better parents because of it. I don't wish infertility on anyone, but I also wouldn't take any of it back. I am proud and happy we went through it, because of where we are now."

Laura and Colin are now 11 weeks pregnant with a baby boy.

"We know that marriage is something that requires work. When we need to be patient, we have to be patient. When we need to be thoughtful, we have to be thoughtful. We have to just be willing to do what is needed in that time."

"*I don't think it is the case where you exchange rings and then you are done. There are going to be highs and lows, and you have to enjoy the highs and know that the lows are not forever.*"

"*They pass. You work through them. Marriage is an active thing. It is not something you passively are a participant in.*"

"We've been married now for over four years and together for over eight years. I thought on our wedding day I couldn't love him more, but I was wrong. Every year, every challenge, every trip together, my love for him grows more and more."

"An amazing marriage is being with someone who you want to share the foxhole with through life's downs, as well as the ups." ♥

"Looking back, it's been a really, really rough year, but I would not change any of it. I have learned so much about myself, and it has made us stronger as a couple. We are going to be better parents because of it. I don't wish infertility on anyone, but I also wouldn't take any of it back. I am proud and happy we went through it, because of where we are now."

JENNIFER *and* BOB

MARRIED 28 YEARS
BERKELEY SPRINGS, WEST VIRGINIA

After living on a sailboat with her family until the age of 17, Jennifer and her family moved to Annapolis, Maryland.

"I went to the Boat Show everyday looking for a guy. Actually, I was looking for a wind surfer, but I was more interested in the guys. I saw Bob and said, 'that is going to be my boyfriend.' I knew immediately. He was gorgeous."

"I was immediately drawn to Jennifer's joie de vivre. I had never met another girl who was interested in doing things. When she expressed interest in wind surfing and doing all these things, I thought 'Wow. This is pretty cool.'"

They quickly learned that they shared a love of sailing and both had sailed across the Atlantic. They shared a special love for the Azores Islands. They were both really into wind surfing and reggae music too.

Four months after Jennifer and Bob started dating, they both enrolled in a community college. "We had a really good time at that school and then we went up to the University of Maryland together. We were both really into starting our own business. With a heavy influence from my dad, we operated a lunch delivery service to all of the boats and the boating industry in Annapolis.

Then the next summer, Bob opened a wind surfing school and I ran the lunch delivery service. So, we were both working really hard and making a lot of money.

"In all, we broke up three times before we got married. At the end of the day, love triumphed over our hurdles."

Jennifer and Bob started their married lives together living in Washington, D.C. working separate occupations. After six years, they realized they wanted to travel.

"We took four years and traveled around the world by bike. That experience had a massive impact on our relationship. Our whole life shifted. We had months and months and months without touch from family. Our reliance on each other made our relationship grow hugely. We were forced to talk to each other about our weakest moments and our deepest fears. I don't think we ever talked that deeply before that trip. Biking through India, where we couldn't relate, there was nothing else to do besides reflect and look at our lives and the lives we lead at home."

"We spent a lot of time in developing countries and realized we didn't need to be spending $2,000 a month in rent just to open our front door. We realized we wanted a slower pace than our D.C. lifestyle. When we came home, Jennifer found this property in West Virginia and we bought it."

"It was hard to transition back to life in the States. It still is. We chose to live in a place as small as we possibly could, as cheap as we could, because we wanted our freedom. We took several intense months of just reflecting and looking through the 18,000 slides we took on the bike trip."

Shortly after their return, they welcomed their first of two sons.

"When we had kids, we had been married for 10 years and had been dating for 16. We had a very strong relationship before they were born, which was huge for us. But, we still noticed along the way, the strain children have on a relationship. It is massive. Wonderful, but massive. We started realizing that everything became about our baby.

We stopped taking care of our relationship, we didn't go on dates, and it definitely wasn't as romantic. We had to make the choice to restart the whole thing. Our good friend told us at one point that we needed to romance a little more, because we would eventually lose it if we didn't. Later in life, when the novelty wears off, you have to do the romance thing again."

"We literally had to put our kids aside at times and be just the two of us again. That was hard for us. We were really intense parents, so we wanted our kids with us at all times. But we had to force ourselves to spend the time together developing our interests that we could ultimately share with one another."

"Both of our parents were excellent role models

for us. They were very committed to each other and always put themselves above everything. Jennifer's parents, growing up in the 60s, were very into communicating their feelings. My parents were more Victorian as far as keeping things repressed. When we have problems, Jennifer forces the issue to communicate and talk about it. Whereas, I would rather just let it sit, and get back to it. But, she forces the issue always."

"We are each other's critic and each other's bolster. He is my strength that allows me to go and do what I want, because I know the support will always be there. Each of us will always be there for the other person no matter what happens. However wacky the dream may be, we always support each other to try wacky stuff. We force ourselves to have fun. It seems weird, because having fun is all that we wanted to do when we were young. But, for some reason, when we get older, we forget to have fun. We all-of-a-sudden have all of this stuff to get done and we forget to have fun."

"There are a few things we go all out on... champagne, coffee, and good food. We celebrate every night

with champagne in our crystal flutes from our wedding day."

"At some point, you just have to say, 'you know what, we have arrived.' It doesn't get any better than champagne and crystal. It is a reminder to ourselves daily that we are here, and now is the time to celebrate."

"An amazing marriage is one where we know what we are doing together is way bigger than what we could do singly. For us, one plus one equals four." ♥

219

"However wacky the dream may be, we always support each other to try wacky stuff. We force ourselves to have fun. It seems weird, because having fun is all that we wanted to do when we were young. But, for some reason, when we get older, we forget to have fun."

JAN *and* LARRY

MARRIED 9 YEARS
MADISON, WISCONSIN

"*Of all the gin joints in the world, Jan had to walk into mine.*" Jan and Larry met at Larry's favorite gin joint while they were each waiting for a table with friends. When Jan's table was ready, Larry's friend had to leave, so she and her friend invited Larry to join them for dinner. At the end of

the night, Jan's friend told her she thought Larry was really nice and recommended that she date him. Jan's response was, "Oh no. He's way too smooth."

"Neither of us was looking for a relationship, but we started seeing each other casually. Over time, we realized how much we enjoyed each other's company. When Larry talked about himself, he talked about his kids, his grandkids, his uncles, and his three brothers. That is how I got to know who he was. Our connection is family. For us, family is one of those values that we didn't recognize at first, but over the years, it has become very clear that family is core in our relationship."

"We dated each other, then we lived together." Jan and Larry were married in 2006. "We ended up with a beautiful blended family of 22 characters; three daughters, three son-in-laws, two sons, and 12 grandkids. We are blessed."

"One of the things that was very, very, important to us was our kids, and not creating an uncomfortable situation for them. Getting to know them and spending time with them was important."

"When I was married the first time, I was 20 years old and I was a very dependent little creature. Over the years, I grew up. For a lot of years, I think I really stifled who I was. I always thought I needed to fit a certain mold. Larry and I are very different, but he is fine with me being who I am."

"*It is sexy to have someone who is smart, pretty, and has a mind of her own. There is something attractive about an independent woman. I have always believed it is important to find reasons to like yourself and others will like you for those reasons too.*"

"Trust is the cornerstone of everything. We always give one another the benefit of the doubt. When there is trust, you never have to worry about anything. We always assume the best intention and start there."

"Laughter is always at the center of what we do together. When we get up in the morning, there is always something to laugh about. When we go to bed at night, there is always something to laugh about. We get up laughing and go to bed laughing. We have fun every day. That's the gift we would like our kids to have with their spouse… to really enjoy each other."

"I feel very blessed that Larry walked into my life. We have a beautiful life. It is exciting to have the opportunity to experience new things together."

"An amazing marriage to us is OURS." ♥

"*Laughter is always at the center of what we do together.*"

LAURA *and* BRIAN

MARRIED 6 YEARS
MUKWONAGO, WISCONSIN

"Life is good. It's amazing how much you can fit into six years of marriage: learning a lot as a new married couple, job changes, new challenges together, moving to a new city, becoming parents, learning how to be role models by making good choices for our kids, and making big life decisions about where our family should be as our kids grow up and start school. It's definitely a fun, exciting, and challenging ride. An amazing marriage is loving life together as a family, being thankful we're healthy, and planning ahead to what we'd love to see ourselves do together." ♥

ALI *and* KEVIN

MARRIED 4 YEARS
JACKSON, WYOMING

Ali, originally from Chicago and Kevin, originally from Connecticut, arrived in Jackson, Wyoming after college with a desire to ski and enjoy the Tetons. They met while working in a restaurant together. Kevin was a line cook and Ali was a waitress. "We ended up dating for about six months and didn't even tell anybody. It was so much fun keeping it a secret. I got to go to work and see the person that I was totally in love with, and it was a secret!"

Ali and Kevin lived together for about a year before Kevin decided to go to Pastry School in Paris. Ali made the move to Paris to be with him. "It was so nerve-racking. I knew Kevin; I lived with him and spent a lot of time with him. But, we were in a totally foreign place with no comfort zones and support systems. All we had was each other, and neither of us spoke French. Being in Paris together was really a bonding experience. It was so wonderful for our relationship."

After completing Pastry School, Ali and Kevin moved to Chicago, and then back to Jackson, Wyoming to open their bakery together. "We were married the same year we started the business. It was the most stressful year ever."

"Opening a business together was certainly the hardest obstacle we have faced. Honestly, I don't think we realized how much work it was going to take to stay connected as a couple and not just business partners. We actually have to make an effort, especially when we are so busy and all that we do is talk and think work. It is hard to leave it at work. We both really love what we do and are so excited about what we are building."

"When you are married, you feel like you have a lifetime together. I think I had in my mind this is the point in our lives where we work. It's hard, but this is what you do. We have a lifetime; we are going to be married forever. But, I am realizing that you can't assume that. We have to be intentional and take every moment we can get, every single day. Everything evolves and everything changes. Without taking time immediately, it may not be forever."

"Life has just gotten harder and harder the bigger the business gets."

"I think a year went by, and we didn't even realize we were no longer connecting as a couple. We felt like we were just business partners. We were not taking time off together. We really needed to make that effort to have a life again that was outside of work. Going home, we have to make a conscious effort to leave work at the door and enjoy our lives together. Once we started focusing on this, we remembered how much we love spending time with each other. Work was just blinding us."

"Working together changes your relationship. The dynamics of who you are and how you

work together changes continuously. It is really important to keep sight of the person that you love, separate from the person that you work with, because it can easily meld into one unrecognizable thing."

"Our favorite thing about being married is having a best friend who will always be supportive, no matter what. It is really special knowing that every day when I come home, there is a person there that wants to hear about my day, will listen to my stupid stories, have a good time, and laugh with me. I am happy just being next to him."

"I never thought I would live in Jackson, Wyoming. I thought I would be in the suburbs of Chicago, like my parents, sending my kids to the same high school, because that is what everybody does. Other plans took me elsewhere. My life is what it is because I met Kevin. I honestly do believe my life is pretty enriched and pretty amazing to be here and be able to do what we have done together."

"An amazing marriage is looking forward to spending time with this person more than anyone else in the universe." ♥

"We have a lifetime; we are going to be married forever. But, I am realizing that you can't assume that. We have to be intentional and take every moment we can get, every single day. Everything evolves and everything changes. Without taking time immediately, it may not be forever."

AFTERWARD

The number of years married, the location, and the details of each couple's story is consistent with the time and location in which we met that couple. Therefore, for many, a lot has happened between then and now. A few of them have provided updates:

RAE AND WES - *We spent exactly two years living in the RV with our three girls. As of December 2016, we moved to a house just a few miles down the road in Santa Rosa Beach.*

JEN AND REUBEN - *We are building a beautiful home, a dream come true after looking for many years for a place to settle with our four children. Prioritizing marriage has resulted in a deeply connected and rewarding relationship, which we are so grateful for.*

SHEFALI AND BRYAN - *Bryan, Shefali, big brother, Noah, and big sister, Pebbles welcomed Nikhil Samuel Lindsey on July 8th, 2016. Our hearts are full.*

CARLY AND BOBBY - *Carly and Bobby welcomed a baby girl, Evelyn Elizabeth, to their family on February 23, 2017.*

DELPHIA AND MATT - *We've since moved back to Southern California and have started our own Marketing Agency focused on Tourism, Hospitality, and Active Lifestyles. It's an area of focus we're passionate about and want to share with the world. There's something really special about being able to love and work together at the same time.*

CHRISTY AND JAMES - *Christy and James welcomed their twin boys to the world in March of 2016.*

AMANDA AND TYLER - *Asher is now two and a half years old and still very energetic. He became*

a big brother to Beckham Joseph Parkhurst on October 26, 2016. Beckham is a very happy and mellow baby. In addition to our family growing, our business is as well. In April, 2017 we will be opening our 3rd cafe. One thing that hasn't changed is how much I love my wife.*

KIM AND JOSH - *Our baby girl, Isadora was born on Thanksgiving, 2015. She's a busy toddler now. Next week, we are moving back to my hometown on the Connecticut shoreline.*

CARIN AND JAIME - *Jaime is now serving another active duty tour at Shaw Air Force Base, in South Carolina. We are being tested, yet again, to survive apart.*

MELANIE AND MARK - *Our family is wonderful! We have been blessed with our first grandchild. He will be two in March.*

RENEE AND REESE - *The only thing that has changed about us is that we now live in Grand Rapids, Michigan.*

TAYLOR *and* JESSE

Taylor and Jesse were one of the very first couples we intereviewed for Amazing Life Together. We hung out with them in their home in Charlotte, North Carolina during a "test run" of the Amazing Marriage Adventure in 2014. Taylor and Jesse blew us away with their zest for life, unbelievable courage, and joy-filled energy.

In December, 2013, during a routine appointment, the doctor found a cyst that lead to Taylor's diagnosis of Ovarian Cancer.

From that moment on, Taylor and Jesse fought hard together with awe-inspiring love. As Jesse said about Taylor during our time with them, "*I don't know if I have ever seen someone handle something so hard with so much grit and so much grace at the same time. That has been so inspiring as a husband to watch on a daily basis.*"

After an incredibly brave battle with Ovarian Cancer, Taylor passed away on November 18, 2016.

Although Taylor and Jesse's story wasn't "technically" a part of the Amazing Marriage Adventure, as are the other stories in this book, their impact on our hearts and the hearts of so many will forever be an awe-inspiring example in our hearts of what it truly means to live an amazing life together. ♥

http://www.amazinglifetogether.com/films/takesoncancer

ACKNOWLEDGEMENTS

This book would definitely not have been possible without the help of so many. It was a true team effort and we are so grateful for everyone who helped make it a reality.

Thank you to all of the couples who have taken the time to share their love story with Amazing Life Together. For all of the couples in this book and beyond, who opened their homes to us, your hospitality and beautiful hearts left an imprint on ours that will never be forgotten.

Thank you to Liz's mom, Tina, and one of our very best friend's, Jenna, for not only editing this book, but offering help throughout the whole process.

Thank you to every single person who has supported Amazing Life Together with your generous donations and/or gifts of time and talents. Without your donations from our Indiegogo Campaigns (your names are on the next page!), we definitely would not have been able to complete the Amazing Marriage Adventure, or this book. You fueled the RV and gave us confidence when we needed it most.

Allison, Tom, Avery, and Logan, it is hard to come up with words to thank you for all that you did for us during 2015 and beyond. You offered us stability when we needed it most. It was such a gift to come "home" to your beautiful house. Getting snowed in with you was our favorite.

Jen, Ryan, Clare, and Jackson, there are not many people who would say yes to adventure the way you all do! Thank you for opening your yard to us and giving us a place to adjust to life in one location again! Those few weeks in Florida with you were truly life-giving. We are forever grateful. Jen, the cover of this book would not be the same without you! Thank you!

To our Amazing Life Together Board of Directors, Allison, Tom, Jim, and Martha, your guidance has been monumental. Thank you for believing in our mission.

To our talented cinematography friends, Lee, Melissa, and the Clickspark/Mozell team, as well as Ashley and Jeremy of We Are the Mitchells, THANK YOU! Not only are you amazing friends, but you helped get this project off the ground before we even knew what it looked like.

To our amazing couples we have had the honor of photographing through our photography business, your love has impacted us in big ways. Thank you for sharing it with us.

Thank you to our family and friends. When we think we are crazy, you confirm that we are crazy and then support us anyway. Thank you for never giving up on us and being there when we need you most.

Karen and Brendon, remember that time we arrived to your house at 11:00 p.m. and then exploded in your kitchen? Thank you for opening your home and embracing our crazy.

To our Well Crafted Pizza business partners and lifelong friends, Laura and Tom, thank you for guiding us through the last two years of our lives! When we did not have it together, you had it together for us! Thank you for dreaming big dreams with us and making them a reality. And thank you for opening your home as well. Yep, we did live with you for six unforgetable months! We are forever grateful!

As you can see, so many people came together to make this Book and the Amazing Marriage Adventure a reality. So many people poured their hearts into it, literally, and that is something we will never forget. We are so grateful for each and every one of you. ♥

INDIEGOGO DONORS

Donors to the Indiegogo Campaigns, who have not chosen to be anonymous, are listed below. Thank You.

A Restored Life
Aaron Griffy
Abbeigh Blake
Abby Grace Springmann
Abi Losli
Alecia & Taylor Zenker
Alex Hinders
Alexandra Young
Alexandria Hinders
Alicia Sturdy
Allen Lorson
Allison & Tom Barnhill
Alyssa Padgett
Amanda Delgado
Amy Wiebe
Andrew Ritter
Ann Pearce
Ann Phillips
Anna Kerns
Arminta McKinney
Ashley & Eric L'Esperance
Ashley & Jeremy Mitchell
Ashley Crosby
Ashley Wondolowski
Becky Morquecho
Becky Stavely
Betsy Watson
Bevin Fritz-Waters
Bob & Barbara McGinnis
Bonnie & Pete Axeman
Brandi Hunley
Briana Elledge
Brigitte & Donald Manekin
Brooke & Kevin Shivers
Brooke & Tony Shurer
Bryan Engels
Cait Engels
Carin Mileshosky
Carin Mileshosky
Carly Grennes
Carol & Dan Fetzer
Casie Turcotte
Cassandra Hansen
Catherine Cravath Thorin
Cathy & Jeff West
Chelsea Tademy
Chris Guillebeau
Christine Olson
Christine Preddy
Christy & James Tyler
Colleen Waterston
Cynthia & Jerry Lorson
Darcy Stanton

Denise Foery
Desiree Ortman
Drew & Rachel O'Brien
Eileen Weinberg
Elizabeth Dusold
Elizabeth Langford
Emily Cooper
Emily Ronsman
Emily Bostic Skorupinski
Emily Wolf
Emmy Gorman
Eric Pearson
Erica Keane
Erica Makos
Erin & Jeff Youngren
Everything Anastacia
Fleetwood Area Public Library
Gina Fitzsimmons
Gina Zeidler
Grace Mackey
Hannah Barber
Hayley Smith
Heather Baker
Jacci Pellett
Janet Hamik
Janet Kirkwood
Jason Partee
Jay Minnick
Josh & Jenny Solar
Jeff Dewberry
Jen Hansard
Jen Logan
Jenn Jett
Jenna Camann
Jenna & Justin Gamerl
Jenna Vince
Jennifer Aguilar
Jennifer Freedman
Jennifer Garbett
Jennifer Ivester
Jennifer Pochobradsky
Jessica Cortes
Jessica Frey
Jessica Wack
Jessica Waltersdorff
Jessie & Mike Shurer
Jessie Emeric
Jeweliet & Joe O'Connor
Jillian Schweitzer
Jim & Martha Wang
Jo & Carl Shurer
Joie Magazine
Jon Shanklin

Josh Grill
Josh Mull
Joshua Holbein
Juliana Massaro
Juliana Neelbauer
Justin & Mary Marantz
Kait & Adam Pecina
Karen & Brendon Raraigh
Karen Rainey
Katey Blauvelt
Kath Bailey
Katherine Arnold
Katie Wondolowski
Kellie & Marshall Chaney
Kellie Karschner
Kelly Newsome
Kelly Pollack
Kristin Stetler
Laura & Tom Wagner
Laura Gainor
Laura Gill
Laura Ruiz
Lauren Girio
Lauren Gonzalez
Lea Ciceraro
Lee Morton
Lindsay Sutton
Lindsey Chambers
Lindy & Jason Weimer
Lisa Madden
Lisa Munzer
Lisa Swoyer
Luke Sheppard
Marianne Bailey
Marty Coyne
Mary Griffy
Matthew Anderson
Mattye Woodcock
Megan Beck
Megan Decker
Megan Esqueda
Megan Miller
Meggie Bennett
Melanie Baunchalk
Melanie Tablante
Melissa Fancy
Melissa Manzione
Melissa McManus
Mia Lycett
Michelle & Bill Kupiec
Mike & Winnie Kremser
Mike Hanline
Minh Hussey

Molly Yearick
Nicole Cole
Octavia Roberts
Pam Butler
Patty & Bob Bower
Philip Niemie
Rachel Harrod
Rebecca Solano Hay
Ron & Kim Lorson
Ronald Frick
Susan Dziurawiec
Sabrina Fields
Samantha Ernst
Sara Moore
Sarah & Eddie Hart
Sarah Stiltner
Scott & Shelly Elston
Scott Courtney
Shannon Fitzpatrick
Shannon Rosser
Sharon Hundley
Shawn Brown
Shefali Lindsey
Sherry & Gary Sandt
Shreya Dasgupta
Sophie & Dave Coates
Spring McKenney
Stephanie & Greg Cully
Stephanie Phaniphon
Stephen & Chelsey Diaz
Steve & Michele Hecht
Stevie Oliver
Suzy & Lukas VanDyke
Sylvester & JoAnn Lucido
Tammy Bashore
Tera & Wes Wages
Terry Hinders
Tina Solak
Todd Watson
Tracey Ciesnolevicz
Traci & Kevin Schultz
Tracy & Joseph Koolick
Trey Phillips
Tyler Parkhurst
Wayne & Janie Newton
Xiomara

MEET LIZ AND RYAN BOWER

Liz and Ryan are storytellers, photographers, dream believers and amazing life inspirers. They are high school sweethearts who grew up in Montoursville, Pennsylvania. After graduating from Bucknell University, they moved to Baltimore, Maryland and started corporate careers. With an entrepreneurial spirit and a passion to live a meaningful life, they started a photography business (Liz and Ryan) in 2009, both working full-time on the business by 2012.

In 2013, Liz and Ryan founded Amazing Life Together, which became a 501(c)(3) non-profit organization in 2014, with a mission to inspire all couples to live a happy, healthy, and everlasting amazing life together.

In January 2015, Liz and Ryan rented out their home in Baltimore, bought an RV, and set out on the Amazing Marriage Adventure, to document at least one married couple's love story in each state. At the completion of the Amazing Marriage Adventure, Liz and Ryan moved back to Baltimore, Maryland where they co-own a Mobile Pizza Kitchen (Well Crafted Pizza) and continue to document love stories.

AMAZING
LIFE TOGETHER

ABOUT AMAZING LIFE TOGETHER

Amazing Life Together is a 501(c)(3) organization with a mission to inspire all couples to live a happy, healthy, and everlasting amazing life together. Founded in 2013 by Liz and Ryan Bower, Amazing Life Together has documented and shared over 100 unique love stories in hopes of opening the lines of communication surrounding marriage and encouraging couples to celebrate life and love after their wedding day.

CPSIA information can be obtained at www.ICGtesting.com
Printed in the USA
LVIW01n2305190417
531472LV00004B/5